PURSUIT of HAPPINESS

By the same author

Homoeopathic Guide to Family Health

Bhartrihari: *Atha Nitishatakam*

Bhartrihari: *Atha Sringarshatakam*

Bhartrihari: *Atha Vairagyashatakam*

How to Stay Healthy with Homoeopathy

Kalidasa: *The Meghadootam*

Kalidasa: *The Ritusamharam*

Kalidasa: *The Kumarasambhavam*

Kalidasa: *The Raghuvamsham*

Krishnaleela and Other Tales from *Shrimadbhagavatam*

Valmiki Ramayana

PURSUIT of HAPPINESS

Made Easy

Rajendra Tandon

BLUEJAY

Bluejay Books Pvt. Ltd.
A-8/76, Ist Floor
Sector 16, Rohini
Delhi 110 085
info@bluejaybooksindia.com

First published in 2013 by
Bluejay Books Pvt. Ltd.

Typeset by EGP

Printed and bound in India

To my daughter Bindu.
She, with her even and joyful temperament, is a perennial source of happiness for me and my wife.

CONTENTS

PREFACE

Even if the world is full of suffering, it costs us nothing to break this logjam and attain a modicum of happiness. In the pages that follow, I have tried to suggest several inexpensive ways to achieve this goal. Each of the suggestions is born out of my personal experiences and can, therefore, be called tried and tested to be successful.

I believe happiness to be our birthright. But one must not forget that all rights are not granted automatically; it requires some effort. The efforts suggested herein – meditation, gentle behaviour, listening to music, bird songs, the ocean's roar, or gazing at the divine sky on a dark night, and admiring the colour and texture of flowers – would cost you nothing. Take this opportunity and dive into the ocean of life and nature in search of lustrous pearls of happiness, available to all and sundry most conveniently.

The pages that follow describe the philosophy of happiness that every religion talks of – the nature of suffering and devised means for its alleviation. Poets, thinkers and naturalists have made significant contribution in understanding the basis of happiness. I have tried to bring their effort to your notice in the form of this manual. I recommend that you participate in this discovery of happiness that lies within; you will not return empty-handed.

I thank my publisher, Mr. Vijay Sharma for accepting this title for publication. I acknowledge the contribution of my editor Ms. Stuti Sharma in tightening the text. I found her observations incisive, bold and extremely helpful.

Rajendra Tandon

January 1, 2013

1

HAPPINESS DEFINED:
CATCHING A BEAM OF LIGHT

The sun and stars that float in the open air;
The apple-shaped earth and we upon it----
Surely the drift of them is something grand!
I do not know what it is, except that it is grand,
And that it is happiness.
—Walt Whitman, *Carol of Occupations*, 1855

HAPPINESS, or *ananda* as it is called in Sanskrit, has been pursued with unending efforts ever since man came to be. Realizing the limitations of this effort, the great Greek tragedian Euripides wrote in 421 B.C., "no one is happy all his lifelong". Yet, human beings constantly strive to achieve happiness because, as Aristotle put it, "Happiness is at once the best, the noblest and the pleasantest of things" (*The Nicomachean Ethics,* 1, c. 340 B.C.).

What is happiness?

Is happiness a mere delusion or is it a substantial experience? Can it be quantified like the possession of wealth? Is it a transient emotion like sexual climax or a longer, more permanent experience like an hour-long performance by Bhimsen Joshi, Kishori Amonkar or Ravi Shankar?

Technically, happiness is defined as a state of mind or feeling characterized by contentment, love, satisfaction, pleasure, or joy.

Absence of sorrow

Happiness is also the absence of sorrow, which in the nature of things is more lasting, more visible than the moments of joy. Since sorrow or suffering cannot be eliminated, seeking happiness becomes vital for survival.

Role of human mind

The secret of overlooking sorrow and achieving an exalted state of happiness lies in our mind, in our thought process. The mind is the villain; the mind is the hero.

When a child gets hurt and cries, the mother's consolation inevitably is, "You are brave, and brave kids don't cry." I have seen every child reacting positively to this consolation because it diverts their mind. The child begins to feel that it is brave and must not cry because weeping is a sign of cowardice. This is the sort of control the mind exercises.

But then, how does one control the mind? Will that necessarily lead to happiness? What are the means to achieve this? Have they been uniformly successful?

The mind is a wanderer. It deviates, more often than not, towards undesirable actions, situations, forces of evil or lust, greed, arrogance and cruelty. Can we pull back the reins? Can we focus on desirable things all the time?

Means to achieve happiness

There are several paths that lead to experiencing happiness: right action, right thought, right concentration and meditation, enjoying nature, listening to music, painting, and looking after the welfare of our fellow beings, among several others.

In my experience, I have discovered a few short-cuts to achieve happiness, even if for a short duration. Out of the many, the paramount one is meditation.

I shall take up a detailed discussion on meditation in the pages that follow. I will try and describe how it has been propounded by Krishna in *Shrimadbhagavata Purana.*

I propose to discuss, in brief, most of the above means to attain happiness and certain others which are available to everyone, without much effort.

Let us embark on a journey into the realm of *ananda,* uninhibited happiness.

> *The art of being happy lies in the power of extracting happiness from common things.*
> —Henry Ward Beecher

2

POSITIVE THOUGHTS:
THINK WELL OF OTHERS

Happiness is that pleasure which flows from the sense of virtue and from the consciousness of right deeds.

—Henry More, *Enchiridion Ethicum*, ii, 1667

MORE has captured the essence of happiness precisely in the above lines. One of the Indian Upanishads features the following *shloka* :

सर्वे भवन्तु सुखिनः सर्वे सन्तु निरामया,
सर्वे भद्राणि पश्यन्तु, मा कश्चित् दुःख भाग भवेत् ॥

It can be translated as:

May everyone be happy!

May everyone be healthy!

May we find everyone prosperous and blessed!

May we see nothing but good in others!

We pray that none suffers even the slightest of pain.

Easier said than done, you might say. Our good wishes are not bearer cheques that can be cashed at will. However, that is precisely the point. Thinking well of others – even of those who apparently act hostile or harbour inimical feelings towards us and others – sends salutary vibrations. A positive modification in your behaviour influences the conduct of the other who might have taken a hostile position.

A change in your feelings might not show instant results. However, in the long run, it surely will. It will result in happiness all around.

POSITIVE THINKING ABOUT OTHERS

How does it work?

On a practical plane, when we think well of others, we act accordingly. The thoughts are translated into action. The person concerned is bound to notice this conciliatory change and shed off his stance as an adversary, after the initial confusion. This approach is effectively illustrated by Rishi Valmiki in the meeting of Rama and Sugreeva.

In the *Valmiki Ramayana,* as Rama and Lakshmana approach Sugreeva's hideout on the Rishyamooka Mountain (Kishkindha Kandam), the latter loses his appetite. He thinks that the two armed warriors are coming at the instance of his brother Vali, to kill him. He is unsure of their intentions. He is restless, frightened and sad as the mere glimpse of the two warriors saps his happiness out. Addressing his companions, he says:

"The two warriors have certainly been sent by Vali. For disguise, they are dressed in bark. They have reached us crossing a thick forest, otherwise difficult to access."

However, Hanuman thinks otherwise. Addressing his king, he says, "Please give up Vali's fear on this mountain. He cannot reach here. O Vanararaja, you are unable to think straight because you are disturbed and restless. You are endowed with wisdom and logical reasoning; try to understand the motives of these visitors from their movements and act accordingly."

Hanuman is sent to negotiate and probe for the truth.

Polite words and behaviour win half the battle

Jumping over rocks, Hanuman arrived at the place where Rama and Lakshmana were resting. He assumed a hermit's form to establish credibility and approached the two. Hanuman humbly bowed to them and spoke in sweet and polite words:

"O brave men, you appear to be truthful, powerful like the gods, hermits and men of a firm resolution. You are so handsome. Masters, what brings you to this forest? Your presence has added to the beauty of the fine trees and made the Pampa lake more attractive than before. Your limbs glow like gold. You look like lions. You are strong enough to destroy your enemies with your bows and arrows. What brings you to this inaccessible place?

"In you, the sun and moon appear to have descended on the earth. Have you come from the Swargaloka? Your bows are gold-plated; the quivers full of arrows deadly as snakes look grand; and your swords are strong, broad and sharp with handles made of gold.

"I represent Sugreeva, a pious and brave vanara who has been thrown out of his home by his brother, Vali. Everyone knows me as Hanuman. I am the son of Pavana, the God of Wind although I am a vanara. At the moment, I am in disguise for the benefit of Sugreeva.

"The pious Sugreeva wants to befriend you. I am his minister and representative."

Addressing Lakshmana, Rama said,

"Sumitranandana, this wise man comes to us as a representative of Sugreeva for his master's benefit. He is perspicacious. Please respond politely and with warmth."

This incident shows the importance of a conciliatory approach, in this case even towards an unknown person. While Sugreeva had his misgivings, Hanuman thought positively and befriended Rama who due to his polite words and manners in due course restored the kingdom to Sugreeva.

Thinking well of others does not require effort

Thinking well of others is a matter of attitude which can be developed. Many of us live with the philosophy that most people around us are good. If we stop awhile and change 'most' to 'all', it will have a relaxing, soothing effect on us. It will change our attitude towards others and we will begin to see virtues even in persons who might appear difficult to comprehend at first.

In our everyday social interactions, happiness is generated by being nice to each other. If the element of formality can be eliminated from a greeting; if with a slight effort, or out of sustained and carefully developed habit, our words exude genuine warmth, a sense of joy is generated. That is happiness.

In a Rotary or Lions Club meeting, one can notice how the art of joyous greetings has been perfected, how everyone displays a delight in meeting friends and fellow members as if he is meeting a long lost friend.

Look at the positive side of a situation,

Positive thoughts need not be restricted to social gatherings alone. What matters is looking at the positive side of a situation wherever it may arise.

It cannot be denied that in human relations at various levels, as also in matters of national importance, there are two aspects to a situation. Looking at the positive aspect makes taking decisions and actions easier and leads to a solution out of a tricky or unhappy situation. Sticking to the negative aspect, on the other hand, would lead only to bitterness.

Take for instance the Tahrir Square revolution in Egypt (January-February, 2011). The protesting crowds stuck to non-violence while agitating for their rights. Even the agent provocateurs riding on camels and horses, carrying unsheathed swords and guns ready to shoot, did not unhinge the peaceful demonstrators. The latter looked at the positive side of their struggle, sure of its sanctity and justification. They stayed put and lived in a carnival atmosphere, with the whole world glued to their television sets, firmly believing in and expecting success in their struggle for freedom from a dictatorial regime. It was positive thinking and action that ultimately brought them success and jubilation.

The Sanskrit *shloka* mentioned a few pages back highlights the recurrence of one word - *sarve*, that is 'all' or 'everyone'. The seeker makes no exception of class, caste or creed. The one who utters this prayer does not bind his world to his kith, kin or countrymen. He, instead, is asking for the boon of happiness for all. In this universality of thought lies the secret of his happiness. His thought encompasses the entire mankind.

Think positively of others: it is a small step, but a significant one. Think positively in difficult situations. Think of your strengths to overcome your weaknesses; that is a sure path to happiness.

While you wish to be a happy person, did you wonder how your own happiness is subtly related to happiness of people around you? If you try to make others happy, you reach your goal automatically.

- Did you say thank you to the liftman this morning? If not, cover up for it the next time. It will make his day.
- Did you smile at the security person when he held the gate open for you? If not, start doing so

tomorrow onwards. The smile on his face will make you smile, too.

- Pay the cabbie with a smile and say 'thank you'. You pay for the service and thank him for generating a happy vibration.
- The last time you went out for a meal, did you tell the restaurant manager and the chef that the food was delicious? Appreciate their food, the decor and the prompt service, if true, and see them beaming with delight.
- Do you carefully consider your words before you offer a compliment? A few carefully chosen and genuine words of appreciation go a long way in lifting even the most sombre mood.

> *The secret of happiness is this: let your interests be as wide as possible, and let your reactions to the things and persons that interest you be as far as possible friendly rather than hostile.*
>
> — Bertrand Russell, *The Conquest of Happiness, x,* 1930.

3

THE BUDDHA'S PATH TO HAPPINESS

> *Thousands of candles can be lighted from a single candle, and the life of the candle will not be shortened. Happiness never decreased by being shared.*
>
> —The Buddha

EVERY religion, be it Buddhism, Christianity or Hinduism, has striven to lead its followers into the realm of bliss. If mankind was not striving to find a path out of the woods of sorrow, suffering, sickness, or tragedy, religious thought would not have developed with the same vigour in the history of human civilization. All religions lead man to realize the transitory nature of pain and the immortality of bliss. It is a promise that can be fulfilled by diverting the sufferer's attention from pain to a higher power, towards practicing good deeds, towards a virtuous conduct and towards truth that lies in the perennial beauty of nature.

The formulations might be different. However, the goal is the same for all religions: to attain god who is truth, bliss and beauty—सत्यम्, शिवम्, सुन्दरम.

The Buddha's journey into eternal bliss

In this journey of mankind towards eternal happiness, Buddhism has played a significant role. Buddha reached enlightenment through realization of the Four Noble Truths, a diagnosis of the human suffering and finding a remedy for the same.

Life is suffering

The First Noble Truth states that birth, old age, sickness, death, sorrow and lamentation, pain, grief, and despair are suffering. Association with the unpleasant is suffering; dissociation from the pleasant is suffering; and to not get what one wants is also suffering.

In a nutshell, life is suffering.

Origin of the suffering: desire

The Second Noble Truth states that the origin of suffering lies in desire or passionate greed. *Vasana* or desire wanders from one pleasure to another, unsatiated. One after the other, it finds fresh delights in newer things such as the pleasures of the senses, thirst for existence and becoming important, and the thirst for non-existence.

Summing up, suffering arises from desires.

Control of desire ends suffering

The Third Noble Truth states that the cessation of suffering can be achieved by the complete cessation of desire or thirst. One has to give up this thirst, renounce it, emancipate oneself from it, and detach oneself from it.

In short, suffering can end if desires are controlled.

Living right brings happiness

The Fourth Noble Truth charts out an eight-fold path which is believed to be the key to the cessation of suffering, and thus, a road to happiness. The Noble Eightfold path directs a person to observe right view; right thought; right speech; right action; right livelihood; right effort; right mindfulness; and right concentration.

It goes to the Buddha's credit and glory that he addressed the most bothersome ailment of mankind, i.e. suffering. Further, he showed a way out of this suffering so that a human being could achieve bliss. The Noble Eightfold Path can be traversed with ease, albeit with determination.

To give up desire is not easy. Mankind survives because it wants to possess land, gold, other human beings, and comforts. While in ascendance, no one wants to accept that even Asoka and Akbar died and their rule ultimately came to an end. A Hosni Mubarak took control of a nation like Egypt, ruled for more than thirty years; yet, he did not want to give up. After forty years of absolute domination over Libya, Gaddafi clung to his throne till he met with an inglorious death. Every prime minister or president, unless barred by law, wants another term. For the dictators, the greed to dominate, to rule others, is insatiable. Look at the man in Uganda who said that those who opposed him will be fed to the crocodiles in Lake Victoria.

A billionaire with a family of less than ten has built a thirty-storey mansion on a hill in Mumbai. How many rooms can he, his wife and children occupy? How many in-house guests can he entertain? From the helipad on his rooftop, one can watch sprawling slums where families consisting of six to eight persons struggle to live in a room of eight feet by ten feet, and that too if they are lucky. There are quite a few who spend their nights on the road dividers or broken pavements under an open sky.

On the other side of the spectrum of riches are Bill and Melinda gates. They have donated one-third of their wealth to charity. In India, Azim Premji of

Wipro has taken a similar step. There are many more walking the path of charity and renunciation with every passing day.

The path of renunciation

Buddha showed man the path of renunciation and the consequent happiness. He, too, was born a prince in the lap of luxury. Yet, in his search for bliss and to put an end to human suffering, he took on the path of renunciation. It is this that leads to non-attachment, and subsequently, happiness.

Renunciation need not mean *sanyasa* or complete abandonment of the world along with its possessions and attachments, or rejection of temporal concerns. That would be running away from life and its responsibilities, besides being impractical. Hermits alone cannot run the show on the earth.

Yet, there are alternatives to live a normal life and yet be unattached. The Buddha was aware of this. He did not want his followers to waste the unique opportunity bestowed upon them in the form of human birth. He wanted them to lead a purposeful life, along with keeping in mind that their thoughts, actions, speech, livelihood, effort, concentration ought to be right or truthful. If this test of being 'right' could be applied to all that was thought and done, the path to eternal bliss would open.

On similar lines, Krishna laid down the principles of Anasakti Yoga in the *Shrimadbhagavatam* and

Bhagavadgita. More of it shall be discussed in detail subsequently.

From the aforesaid discussion it is clear that most important of the Four Noble Truths is the second one that lays down desire as the origin of suffering. The word used in Buddhist texts to describe desire is *trishna*, literally thirst. It also refers to a strong desire. The cessation of this *trishna* brings tranquillity of mind and contentment.

Thomas Wilson wrote the same from a Christian point of view. He says: "the fewer desires, the more peace" (*Maxims Piety and Christianity*, c. 1755).

Overpowering lust

Look deep and you will realize that the Buddha has caught the essence of unhappiness in formulating this edict. One has to rise above *trishna* (thirst/ desire) in order to attain *ananda* (happiness/ bliss).

A parable would befit the usage of this noble truth in everyday life. It is known that moths are attracted to a flame, which leads them to their death. Similarly, human beings rush thoughtlessly into satisfying their desires, good or bad, and destroy their peace of mind. The instance of a mighty king from the *Ramayana* serves to elaborate the point further. Ravana was a valorous king who brought his kingdom to destruction and lost his own life lusting after Sita, a chaste woman and another's wife. It was an irrational desire to begin with, and it led him to his doom. On the battlefield, after Ravana's death, queen Mandodari lamented and confessed Ravana's shortcoming that led to his inglorious death thus:

> "My master, you had conquered the world
> Because you had conquered your senses.
> Out of enmity, those desires
> Have now taken revenge and defeated you.
> Rakshasaraja, all of a sudden you lusted for Sita and
> That led to the destruction of your magnificence,
> Your riches, your body and your kith and kin.
> You had lost your wisdom.
> Your lust made your thinking opaque."

Desire killed Ravana. Desire kills our peace of mind. Desire and happiness are like the two extreme ends of a pole. So the Buddha says, "shun *trishna* for sensual pleasures, for rebirth, and for freedom from the cycle of birth and death. Eschew other subtler forms of desire that arise from sight, sounds, smells, taste, tactile stimuli, and thoughts."

Running in search of a mirage

The word *trishna* has been associated with and forms a part of many Hindu concepts as well. Once such is *mrigatrishna* [*mriga* (deer) + *trishna* (desire)], metaphorically referring to chasing a mirage. The word is also linked to the story of the golden deer which was a turning point in the annals of the *Ramayana*.

Ravana, the king of Lanka, wanted to abduct Sita because he lusted for her body. He persuaded his general, Maricha to assume the form a golden deer in order to entice Rama and Lakshmana away from their cottage.

When Sita's greed overcame her discretion

Ravana instructed Maricha to create an insatiable desire in Sita's mind so that she compells Rama to chase the golden deer.

Valmiki describes how in a short while, Maricha took the form of a golden deer and started ambling in front of Rama's cottage. The top of his horns shone and looked blue like sapphire. His face was freckled by white and black dots. It was lotus red and his ears were lotus blue. He had a long neck and a blue belly. His hinds were creamy white and shaped like the *mahua* flowers. The golden tone of his skin was the colour of the saffron filament. His body was sleek and had an attractive glow. His hoofs reflected light like lapis lazuli; his legs were thin and his tail had the colour of a rainbow.

'The golden deer was grazing in front of Panchavati. At times, he walked away and then returned to draw attention. He played, jumped and rolled in the ground. He joined the other herds but invariably came back keen to invite Sita's attention. He jumped like an acrobat whenever he neared Sita.

Videhanandini Sita, the one with intoxicating eyes, while plucking flowers and walking through the *kanera* bushes and ashoka and mango trees, happened to look at the golden deer. She noticed that his entire coat was dotted with spots shaped like pearls and precious stones. The fur on his skin stood like thin threads of silver and copper.

She was astonished to see the unusually beautiful animal. Sita called Rama and Lakshmana to have a look at the exceedingly charming animal. Lakshmana cast a glance and declared that he suspected deceit and that this deer could be Maricha, the *rakshasa* who could change his form at will.

However, Sita's discretion had vanished with her fascination for the golden deer. She insisted that Rama ensnare it and bring it to their cottage for their entertainment. She said,

"Rajan, although our ashrama is visited by several herds of sacred and pretty deer, some of a variegated coat, as well as by cows with black or white tails, by bears, and by monkeys, I have so far never seen a superior deer like this one, so quiet, glorious and colourful.

"It is an animal of indescribable beauty. It bellows sweetly. Its unusual limbs have won over my heart. It stands fearless in front of me. It illuminates the forest like the moon.

"You ought to catch this deer alive. At the end of our exile, we shall take it along to Ayodhya where it will enhance the charm of our palace. Its divine looks will please Bharata and my mothers-in-law. In case you cannot catch it alive, I shall use his golden skin as a seat.

"I know I am being selfish. A pious woman must not goad her husband in her self-interest to do such a job. However, its astonishing body has excited my curiosity."

Rama himself was astonished looking at the sapphire horns, the glow of the rising sun and spots like those of the star-spangled firmament of the golden deer. Urged by Sita and overexcited on his own, he said to Lakshmana,

"See, how strong is her desire to catch this deer! It is, in fact, an extraordinarily charming animal. It will not live for long. The hairy fur on its spotted skin is fascinating; its tongue protrudes like a flame when it yawns; it shines like lightning; its mouth looks like a bowl made of blue rock; and its belly is fair like seashells or pearls. Such an animal will not be found even in Indra's Nandanavana or Kubera's Chaitraratha forest.

"The skin of no other animal can be as attractive and pleasing to touch as the skin of this golden deer. There are only two divine deer in this category: one is the constellation, Orion in the sky and the other is this spotted golden deer. Even if, as you say, it has been created by *maya* by some *rakshasa,* I ought to kill this animal in order to destroy the illusion of an evil daitya.

"Lakshmana, dressed in full armour, you safeguard Sita while I go to catch this animal, dead or alive. Notice how keen she is to get this deer or its skin. Be very careful in my absence. I shall return soon with the trophy."

This was '*mrigtrishna,*' a compelling desire for a mirage though everyone knows that a golden deer just cannot be. Rama lost his discretion in fulfilling his wife's desire. Sita was overpowered by the idea of possession. This surrender of discretion to desire led to her abduction by Ravana and the consequent unbounded strife and unhappiness.

Ajamil's surrender to sensual pleasures

In the *Shrimadbhagavata Purana,* one reads about Ajamil, a learned brahmin well-versed in Vedas and scriptures. He was an embodiment of nobility, good behaviour and virtue, yet untouched by pride. He cared for his wife and children.

One fine morning, Ajamil, at his father's instance, went into the forest on the outskirts of the city to collect fruit, flowers, holy *kusha* grass, and *samidha* for performing a *havana*. On his way back, Ajamil noticed a drunkard shamelessly making love to a prostitute under a wayside tree. The woman too had imbibed liquor. Her eyes were wild with lust. Her clothes were in disarray. The couple was singing lewd songs and making unseemly conversation.

Ajamil forgot his training and restraint. As he looked at the couple, he could not take his eyes off the half-naked woman. His lust was ignited and he lost his discretion and wisdom. Subsequently, he sent the prostitute a message requesting a meeting and soon, they became lovers. Ajamil carried to her lovely, expensive clothes made of Chinese silk. He presented her with gold ornaments studded with precious stones. He wanted to please her at any cost. In buying her gifts, he squandered his father's wealth for her delight.

Ajamil had forgotten his dharma. To support his mistress's large family, he started borrowing money from others, pawned his wife's ornaments, gambled, looted wayfarers and even committed thefts. He cheated those who trusted him and it was Ajamil's wife and children who suffered as a consequence of his derelict behaviour.

This instance brings us back to the Third Noble Truth: The cessation of suffering lies in the complete cessation of *vasana* (desire or thirst). One has to give up this thirst, renounce it, emancipate oneself from it, and detach oneself from it.

In short, suffering can end if desires can be controlled.

However, one wonders if desire is always evil? The Buddha and other enlightened masters have provided practical answers to this question that have been taken up in greater detail in the following chapter.

> *Not going naked, nor matted hair, nor dirt, nor fasting, nor sleeping on the ground, nor rolling in the dust, nor sitting motionless can purify one who has not overcome desire.*
>
> —*Dhammapada*, x, c. 100

4

TRISHNA AND THE NOBLE EIGHTFOLD PATH

THE PATH OF MODERATION

> *Dwell not upon thy weariness, thy strength shall be according to the measure of thy desire.*
>
> — Arab proverb

Can trishna be negated?

TRISHNA or desire is a quality that cannot be negated in its entirety. How do you ask a human being not to indulge in the simple pleasures of enjoying a delicious meal, putting on nice clothes, participating in sports or attending music or dance performances? Even a mendicant or *sanyasi* who renounces the life of a *grihastha* might give up some of these activities, yet not entirely. If you consider the lifestyles of most of the cult gurus of the present age, you will notice a life of unimaginable luxury. Their ashrams with golden pillars, a fleet of enviable super-luxury automobiles and diamond-studded trinkets are enough proof of their renunciation. And despite all this, fawning disciples lick the guru's feet who sits on a throne of gold. Think of what Acharya Rajneesh had to undergo in the United States of America.

Most such gurus are knowledgeable, and their sermons are a pleasure to read. It seems they forget their own sermons and teachings temporarily as they try to spread happiness in their disciples through knowledge.

Rajneesh (11 December 1931 – 19 January 1990) was one of the finest thinkers of the twentieth century, a man well-versed in literally every religion of the world. He led his disciples on paths which were philosophical, scientific, psychoanalytical, and religious. His knowledge of the West was as formidable as his knowledge of the East. From the Buddha to Jesus, from Heraclitus to Marx, from the Indian mystic Tilopa to Jung, from Zen to the Sufis, from Yoga to Tantra, he would point out the strengths and weaknesses of each doctrine. Hounded out of India, the guru moved to Oregon in USA. He bought a ranch named Rajneesh Puram. It was here that the Acharya, who had called himself Bhagwan, lived a life of luxury. Dressed in velvet and silk robes and diamonds, he moved in a Rolls Royce.

The guru had temporarily forgotten the teachings of the Buddha. He made a showpiece of himself while he was in reality an ascetic, original in thought and deeds. It is a pleasure to read his sermons; his thought output was incredible. However, somewhere, the Acharya lost his path. *Trishna* overpowered him. And with that, he lost whatever happiness he had gained and could disseminate.

Thus, one can say that a moderation of desire is the key to happiness, at all times.

How to exercise moderation?

This brings us to an essential question as to how this can be done. It is like reining the horses of the Sun.

To eschew *trishna,* to the extent possible, the Buddha provided guidelines with precise pointers. The Eightfold Path describes the 'right' measures of eight essential activities which are as follows: right view; right thought; right speech; right action; right livelihood; right effort; right mindfulness; and right concentration. The word 'right' can refer to various things in this context, i.e. that which is just, morally good, legal or proper; a straight and accurate path, in accordance with fact, reason or truth; conforming to justice, law or morality; and reasonable or desirable.

Let your conscience be your guide

Thus, there is an undercurrent of a conscious, moral decision in the word 'right'. It is based on the belief that our conscience invariably guides us towards what is right and desirable under a particular set of circumstances. To our conscience is assigned the task of keeping us walking the straight path.

Conscience is the part of superego in psychoanalysis that judges the ethical nature of one's actions and thoughts and then transmits such determinations to the ego for consideration. Conscience is, thus, awareness of the moral or ethical aspect to one's conduct which determines our preference for the right over wrong. That is why we often hear, 'let your conscience be your guide'.

The Buddha's formulation of the right path has a moral, ethical basis and is in conformity with the call of the conscience. His emphasis on these actions in order to bring an end to *trishna*, the root cause of suffering, seems practical in today's world.

Dukha (suffering) is whatever is painful, disagreeable and unpleasant in life. It is sorrow, grief, unhappiness, misery, distress, pain or agony. The root cause of it all is *trishna*.

Fight trishna by walking the Noble Eightfold Path

Ravana, or even Hitler for that matter, failed the test of the Eightfold Path. Their thoughts were impure;

their deeds heinous. Their effort was inspired by arrogance. Ravana thought he could subdue the willpower of any woman; Hitler thought that he and his race were morally superior to all others. This was certainly not right mindfulness. Their point of view was not right, rather was distorted. They killed their conscience, because the others' suffering meant nothing to them. It fed their megalomania if others died fighting for them. They were obsessed with grandiose, or extravagant things and actions. They were impelled by delusional fantasies of wealth, power or omnipotence.

Ravana lost his brothers and sons on the battlefield and was himself slain at the end. Hitler's Germany waged a war that led to the death of millions of soldiers and civilians besides the destruction of cities. Innocent men and women were among the victims in both cases. Had Ravana and Hitler not strayed from the right path, the carnage would have been avoided.

President Bush's decision to attack Iraq in 2003 proved futile because even after ten years into this invasion, Iraq knows no peace. Bin Laden's hyenas murdered thousands of innocents in their attack on the World Trade Centre in 2001. Peaceful protesters were killed in the Tiananmen Square in Beijing in 1989. These instances are a few consequences of someone's desire or *trishna* for unlimited power.

Right-mindfulness and following the tenets of 'right' as laid down in the Noble Eightfold Path could have avoided these misadventures.

Happiness lies in subduing *trishna* and diverting one's mind and deeds towards common good. That is what one witnesses in struggles against tyranny, where many come together to fight for a common cause. That was the essence of Mahatma Gandhi's *satyagraha,* a philosophy propagating non-violent resistance. How well has his idea succeeded in the struggle of the Egyptian masses in the Tahrir square! The Buddha would have approved of their choosing the path of the right view, the right speech, right action and right concentration. In instances such as these, we notice how happiness does not take birth in vacuum. It is generated by events, by deeds thought out for common good.

The devastating sweep of unbridled desire

Vasana is a Sanskṛit term used for desires of the body, i.e. lust. One should not be judgmental about sexual activity, because in its proper context, it is not only desirable but also necessary for the survival of mankind. However, uncontrolled *vasana* for another's woman leads to disaster, suffering, and unhappiness. Reports had appeared recently about a Prime Minister in Europe who had been charged with having had paid sex with an underage woman. Reportedly, he had been participating in orgies. This is neither right thought, nor right conduct, nor right view.

An unbridled desire develops like foam and engulfs its maker. The neighbour's wife is coveted not because she is necessarily better looking than one's own, but because she is different. She is bound to be different. No two women, or for that matter men, are born in a similar design of handsomeness and beauty. A right thought will take care of the situation. How can a person covet and snatch what belongs to another? Freedom of action does not mean freedom to snatch, to usurp or to waylay another human being or another's property. A violation of this principle invariably leads to unhappiness.

The attitude of a person who desires what belongs to another, is warped. It is his desire overtaking his conscience, his judgment, his wisdom and his mindfulness. He overlooks the virtues of what belongs to him and is, therefore, easily lost in the web of his own desires.

All desire must be moderated and tested on the touchstone of conscience, of ethics and morality before it is fulfilled. That alone will preserve happiness.

> *There is no other way by which the individual can attain his own happiness than that which leads to the common happiness of all.*
>
> — Richard Cumberland, *De Legibus Naturae*, 1, 1672

5

MORAL VALUES

To enjoy and give enjoyment, without injury to yourself or others: this is true morality
— Nicolas Chamfort, *Maximes et Pensées,* c 1785

The bond between happiness and morality

HAPPINESS is intimately linked with morality, so the Buddha believed. According to the Buddhist tenets, morality is based in love for everyone, which in turn leads to satisfaction and happiness. The Noble Eightfold Path wanders through the fields of morality, of moral values, with bliss being the destination.

The essence of morality

The word 'morality' means the quality of being in

accordance with standards of right or good conduct. That is what the Buddha preached and practised. For him '*sheela*' or morality implied the right human behaviour in action, speech and livelihood. The right action is not killing, stealing or harming other beings; the right speech does not hurt others. The right livelihood does not deprive anyone else of what is his due. Positively pursued, these moral practices make both the practitioner and all others happy.

If a person does not intentionally destroy life, does not steal or tell a lie, does not sexually molest a victim, does not lie nor imbibe liquor, there would not be an occasion for those with whom he interacts to be unhappy.

Take for instance the action of an antisocial force. Every terrorist who destroys himself as a human bomb, kills and maims several innocent others. He destroys the happiness of their fathers, mothers, wives, and children. His intentional act of destroying life goes against the moral values preached by all religions, leading to varied forms of pain, destruction and hence, unhappiness.

Happiness is a sum total of several acts and thoughts

Going by the belief of moral actions being intertwined with happiness, one can divide happiness to exist on two levels – individual and social. On the individual level, it can refer to a person, a family, or a community. And it is only with the cumulative individual happiness that social happiness can be achieved. Even if a few factors stand as stumbling blocks in the path of happiness, it can hamper the entire social milieu.

A tragedy of the nature mentioned in a preceding paragraph is not of the making of anyone except the terrorist; the others were merely victims. It comes unannounced and clouds their happiness. A conscious pursuit of happiness on the level of an individual excludes such conduct and thus, the consequent large scale suffering.

Similarly, foregoing moral responsibilities with respect to the body also leads to unhappiness. As discussed in the previous chapter, Ajamil lost his sense of morality and gave in to sensual pleasures, leading to a broken family and the resultant suffering and pain. Thus, chastity can be seen as one rock against which the moral values of a lot of human beings crash. The resultant chaos leads to unlimited unhappiness.

Does a thief feel happy when he breaks open the locks of a jeweller's shop and makes away with a horde of gold and diamonds? Forget the unhappiness and gloom of the jeweller; the thief loses sleep because he fears arrest at any time. His happiness on his acquisition is temporary. What joy can be derived by the person who whisks a Picasso away from a fortified museum? His act makes a thriller worth watching in a cinema. However, his garnering happiness is out of question. All such misdeeds attract severe penalties, which inevitably result in sadness.

All immoral deeds necessarily hurt someone and make the victim unhappy in one way or another. If one considers the case of an obsessed stalker who shot a young woman in public for his liking for her not having been reciprocated, we notice how his immoral and beastly act has caused a permanent scar and deprivation on the victim's family and friends. A charming life has been extinguished for no fault of hers. The cold-blooded criminal faces capital punishment. But in the entire episode, there is no one who has gained happiness.

A lack of morality takes several forms, so does an immoral act.

Another befitting example of how moral degradation hampers happiness and escalates misery is the recent arrest of the managing director of a large government enterprise on account of corrupt practices. He and his wife were found in possession of gold worth millions of rupees, and unaccounted cash and property beyond their known sources of income. Evidently, the accused had flouted all possible norms of morality to acquire wealth of such proportions. He took bribes, cheated the government and his employer in more ways than one, i.e. appointing agents, and distributing favours against rules. He had been recognized as an exemplary chief executive officer of his company a few months ago. Moral values are not writ large on anyone's face, after all. For a long time, this person had walked the swamp of immoral deeds vis-a-vis his conscience. But his ultimate destination would not be happiness, riches or power as he would have visualised, but a strict punishment under the Indian Penal Code. His having forgotten his duty and morality not only took away his position and prestige, but also took a toll on his family life, and his reputation in the long run. Thus, we see, immorality and happiness stand at opposite poles.

It is immoral to ignore the call of conscience

Immorality or the lack of morality takes many forms. Let us take a case from the *Mahabharata* to elaborate upon the point. The most poignant episode in the epic is that of Draupadi's disrobing. The Kaurava king, his princes, collaborators and even the gurus and advisors emerge out of this episode mired in ignominy.

The setting for this episode was the royal chamber for playing dice in the Indraprastha Palace. In the running conflict between the Pandavas and Kauravas, the latter had induced the eldest Pandava, king Yudhishtira, to come to Hastinapur to play a game of dice. Under a scheme devised by Kauravas' maternal uncle Shakuni, they were to trick Yudhishtira into betting his entire kingdom and eventually losing the game of dice to Duryodhana, making the Kaurava crown prince supreme.

The game of dice was being witnessed by all elderly members of the court. King Dhritrashtra's cousin and advisor Vidura was aware of the plot to deprive the Pandava of their kingdom, wealth and prestige.

The Pandava king suffered one loss after another. Forgetting all principles of morality, he bet his brothers and even queen Draupadi when he was left with nothing else to wager. What followed broke all bounds of moral behaviour.

The king did not intervene against his daughter-in-law being used as wager; she was dragged into the court and humiliated. Though she was also the co-wife of the Pandava princes, and Yudhishtira could not have taken this decision without the consent of others, yet, he did so! Bhishma, the grandfather did not bestir himself. He had a strange notion of his loyalty to the throne of Hastinapur and to the king. Both the gurus present did not utter a single word at this immoral act. Vidura alone opposed, but was shouted down by Duryodhana.

Draupadi refused to come for she was menstruating and could not appear in front of a royal gathering in a single piece of cloth. However, Duryodhana crossed all bounds of decency and morality as he sent his younger brother Dushasana to fetch her, even drag her by her long tresses.

Draupadi arrived in this gathering of kings, princes, gurus and elders. The place had been reduced to an immoral den of horrors. Dressed in just a sheet, she was dragged and thrown almost naked before men who looked at her like animals salivating at their prey.

Draupadi challenged each man present in the court, including her husbands who sat with heads lowered. Bhishma did not interfere. The king loved his sons so much that he shut his eyes to the demands of morality and proper conduct. The helpless woman was humiliated and almost disrobed till Krishna helped her through his *maya*.

In India, morality never met with a more inglorious death.

And we all know the consequences of this one immoral deed. What followed was the fierce Mahabharata war and unhappiness. The great clan of heroes was reduced to a few survivors. The wails of the widows from both the camps can still be heard in the pages of the epic.

This brings us to an essential component of decision-making – choice! We often face the twist and turns of the *Mahabharata* in our lives as well. And we make our choices. It is these choices that determine our conduct. Remember the Buddha's insistence on the right thought, right conduct, right word and right choice. Let your conscience be your guide.

> *It is God's will, not merely that we should be happy, but that we should make ourselves happy. This is the true morality.*
>
> — Immanuel Kant, Lecture at Konigsberg, 1775

6

MEDITATION:

AN UNLIMITED RESOURCE OF HAPPINESS

We meditate so that we rise above our visible environment . . . To enjoy true happiness we must travel into a very far country, and even out of ourselves.

— Thomas Browne, *Christian Morals,* 1680

Meditation as a source of happiness

IN the Buddha's scheme of happiness through the Noble Eightfold Path, the right effort, right mindfulness and right concentration relate to 'meditation'. Here, it refers to 'concentration' in order to keep the wandering mind under control.

When we say that a person is sitting in meditation, we imply that he is concentrating his mind on something sublime, on an object that can be visually a source of delight, or on plain nothingness.

One might wonder how can an internal, personal practice, done without any external involvement, lead to happiness? It is possible because meditation often involves 'right-mindfulness' in making a conscious effort to curb or banish undesirable thoughts. 'Mindfulness' is concentrated attention; it might be directed towards a person, an object, a natural phenomenon, or towards 'nothingness'. It is the last that leads to best results in meditation or '*samadhi*'.

Buddhism prescribes several ways to meditate; one of them is *vipassana* and is seen as a stepping stone to seeing the true nature of reality. In this form of meditation, the individual is to sit with eyes closed, in reasonable physical comfort, and focus his mind on the inhaling and exhaling breath, or on the phenomenon of breathing.

When undesirable thoughts or images are banished, the mind wanders in search of 'nothing'. It takes time to achieve this state of detachment from worldly things. However, the effort succeeds with practice. I write this from personal experience: a few minutes into meditation, and a sensation of calm takes over. The load of worries is shed off. If this is not 'happiness', what else can be?

Precise instructions: how to meditate

In *Shrimadbhagavatam,* Krishna tells Uddhava how to meditate. His instructions are precise and easy to follow.

Uddhava, a kinsman, ever in search of wisdom, asked Krishna,

"O Shyamsundara, enlighten me how a seeker, in search of salvation, ought to meditate upon you, in what form, with what ritual, and with what motive?"

Shri Krishna replied, "Dear Uddhava, the seeker ought to sit on a seat that is not high, nor low, yet is comfortable. He should sit straight, comfortably, at ease, placing his palms in his lap. His eyes should focus on the tip of his nose."

The function of breath control in meditation

"To begin with, he has to do *pranayama* involving three quick steps: *poorak, kumbhak,* and *rechak.* This is done in order to control one's breath. *Poorak* is performed by closing the right nostril and inhaling air through the left. Then follows *kumbhak* in which the breath is held for as long as the body comfortably can by keeping the mouth closed and both nostrils closed with the fingers of the right hand. *Rechak* follows *kumbhak* and involves exhaling the held breath through the nostril other than the one used for inhaling. Breath control in this manner establishes peace of mind and improves blood circulation.

"*Pranayama* has to be learnt gradually. Simultaneously, an effort has to be made to overcome sensual desires.

"Inhale deeply and exhale uttering the Om sound as if it is an echo, prolonging the exhalation as much as comfortable. The sound should be deep and sonorous and should not break. Make it melodious and smooth.

"Pranayama should be repeated three times a day, ten times in each sitting. It takes about a month to master one's control over breath."

Visualization

Krishna continues,

"*Pranayama* should be followed by visualization. Think of your heart as a lotus, upside down. Visualize that the lotus has turned upwards and is in full bloom. Look at its petals and the delicate, yellow filaments in the centre. Think of the sunlight, the moonbeams and the light from a fire, in succession, illuminating the yellow core. It is auspicious to think of me while concentrating upon the glow of Agni on the flower.

"I have shapely limbs. Every inch of my body oozes peace. My face resembles a flower in rich bloom. I have long arms; a shapely, delicate neck. My cheeks are smooth like polished crystal and my smile is unique.

"My body is dusky like a rain cloud. A yellow covering flutters on my limbs. On my chest are visible the marks of Lakshmi and Shrivatsa. In my hands I carry a conch shell, a *chakra,* a mace and a lotus. Around my neck I wear a garland of wild flowers. On my feet I wear anklets and my neck is adorned by the Kaustubha gem.

"On my body the *Bhakta* notices a glorious crown, bracelets, ornaments on the upper arms, and a stunning waist band. A contemplation of my captivating looks is most auspicious and helps in concentration. It is a blessing to be able to think of me and of my divinely captivating looks."

Have a focal point

"A wise man ought to exercise control over sensory pleasures through his mind. Assisted by his mind, he can concentrate his thoughts in me. Whenever his attention wanders, he can bring it back by concentrating on my image. He can focus his attention on my smiling visage to the exclusion of all other parts of my being.

"Once the *sadhaka* is transfixed in my blissful visage, he can wander over the skies in search of the absolute. He will revert to me and stay focussed.

"Once there is absolute concentration, like one *jyoti* merging into another, the devotee shall find me and his self submerged into one another and become a part of the universal consciousness.

"Any *yogi* who follows the path of this *dhyana-yoga* and tunes his thoughts to me to the exclusion of all else, overcomes the illusion of diversity among all that is there in the universe." [1]

Meditation, a universal path to happiness

Meditation leading to happiness is not a dry, tedious path. This path has been followed in almost all the religions of the world. We have discussed its importance in Hinduism and Buddhism above.

Jainism

Jainism has stressed upon the practice of meditation right from the beginning of the faith. Mahavira practised deep mediation for twelve years before he achieved enlightenment. For the Jains, meditation is a path to *mukti* or salvation. Salvation is the ultimate bliss because thereafter a human being is not subject to sorrow. Jainism aspires to reach salvation through meditation and continue to be in pure consciousness untouched by avarice, greed, or attachment.

---

1 Krishna's sermon quoted from Tandon, Rajendra. *Krishnaleela.* New Delhi: Rupa & Co, 2012.

Jainism uses, like other religious belief systems, silent contemplation as well as vocal chanting while meditating.

Christianity

In Christianity, the ultimate end of human existence consists in felicity or 'blessed happiness'. Padre Pio, a believer in Christian meditation put it in thoughtful words thus: "Through the study of books one seeks God; by meditation one finds him".

In Christian meditation the worshipper concentrates on specific thoughts and tries to find the presence of God in them. He might think of the young Jesus in Mary's lap or the adult Jesus on a crucifix. The ultimate aim is to sublimate his thoughts to find love and compassion, the pathways to human happiness.

Meditation also leads one to do deeds that bring happiness. For instance, if you are kind to others in your conduct towards them, you will be happy beyond measure. Human acts like charity and compassion make the doer happy.

Islam

Prophet Mohammad spent long periods in meditation, sitting in isolation. His contemplation was rewarded by the revelation of the *Qur'an* that became the holy book and guide to the Muslims. Believers attain happiness by repeated reading and chanting the verses from the holy *Qur'an*.

The Muslims pray five times a day – before sunrise, at noon, in the afternoon, after sunset, and at night. The worshipper concentrates on God while reciting the holy verses. This contemplation gives him peace of mind and happiness. It strengthens his resolve to live a life of peace, charity and good neighbourliness. These feelings are supposed to guide him to a humane conduct in life and goad him towards piety. While praying to God, the believer seeks the truth that links him to God. This effort in itself is ennobling, and acting upon its essence brings him peace of mind and soul, i.e. happiness.

Sikhism

Sikhs live in a tradition of piety and sacrifice. All over the world, in their Gurudwaras, free meals are served to any visitor without distinction of caste, creed or religion. I have been to several such *langars*, the most memorable being the Makindu Gurudwara situated on the Nairobi-Mombasa highway in Kenya. Hot breakfast and meals are served to anyone who drops in. There are no charges. This too is a means of spreading happiness.

Besides, the Sikh Gurus advised meditation to achieve peace inside and outside the body. They asked their followers to concentrate on god's name in order to generate positive emotions. They did not ask their followers to take *sanyasa* to achieve liberation or bliss. They asked them to live a normal life and spread happiness through righteous conduct and working for everyone's welfare.

Japa or *kirtana* was advocated as a means of meditation. Chanting is popular in almost every religion as a means of rising above the turmoil that surrounds us.

Meditation is, thus, at the core of every religious pursuit. Each time, the purpose is attaining bliss by rising above the mundane and the distracting.

Apart from various belief systems and their ways of meditation, there are certain everyday tasks that can lead one to happiness, and also serve as meditative.

Imagine losing yourself in the brilliant spark of star Sirius in the sky, or listening to a cuckoo's song, and the rising notes in her calls. These are all meditative in some sense as they become the centre of our attention and produce a sense of calm. Certain other things that can be similarly categorised include: the beauty of nature in form of flowers or fresh leaves, glistening after a mild shower; the colours of the sky at dawn and sunset; the timely ebb and fall of the ocean waves on a beach and the bass notes of a musical instrument or a soothing song. All these and many other everyday things that escape our attention can be a source of immense joy.

> *Happiness is a mystery, like religion, and should never be rationalised.*
>
> — Gilbert Chesterton

7

HAPPINESS FOR THE AGNOSTICS AND ATHEISTS

Happiness of an atheist is neither the vacuous enjoyment of a fool, nor the short-lived pleasure of a rogue. It is rather the expression of a disposition that has ceased to torture itself with foolish fancies, or perplex itself with useless beliefs.

— Chapman Cohen, "The Happy Atheist", 1987

HAPPINESS is a state of mind where there is a complete absence of thought; and meditation gets you there.

As against popular belief, one need not be religious to meditate. You can attain happiness in meditation even if you are not a believer, because meditation is a way of concentration; it need not necessarily be rooted in belief.

Meditation and religiosity

Even those who are non-believers can be categorised in two ways: agnostic and atheist. The former believes that it is impossible to know whether there is a God. He is non-committal. The latter denies or disbelieves the existence of God.

Either of them can attain happiness through meditation. Meditation need not be linked to a particular religion or belief. On the other hand, it is intimately linked to our breath. Once we concentrate on our breath, it leads to an absence of thought. That is the ultimate purpose of blissful meditation.

Control of breath

The phrase 'control of breath' might seem difficult at first, but it is not. During meditation, one does not so much control breath as concentrate on the sound of its inflow and outflow. Here are a few easy steps to do that, garnered from personal experience.

- Select a suitable time of the day, whether morning or evening, when you have thirty minutes to spare. Make sure to maintain a daily routine of the same.
- Sit in a comfortable chair with a straight back, your feet resting on the ground.

- Loosen your arms and place the palms in your lap. Your body ought to be totally relaxed; no physical tension should act to distract you for that half an hour.
- Relax; forget the worries of the world. Try to get over mental tensions, if any.
- Your room should be dark. Draw the curtains, switch off the lights.
- Disconnect the phone and switch the mobile to silent mode.
- It adds to the overall atmosphere if your room is furnished with scenic images. Do not take a meal or a heavy snack immediately before you sit to meditate.
- During the first week, for the first five minutes, with eyes shut, practice inhalation and exhalation as deep as you can. As you get used to this exercise, you will start breathing deep automatically. It is a matter of time to perfect this art essential to successful meditation.
- While breathing in and exhaling, concentrate on the sound of your breath to the exclusion of all else.
- When you sit to meditate, your mind will wander and try its best to deflect your effort, take you away from what you propose to do. The mind will recall the tensions of the day, the love affairs

of a long time ago, enmities long forgotten, suffering undergone, the recent show down with your boss or the treatment of your colleagues or subordinates, pleasant or unpleasant. Use the same mind as a steering wheel, call it will-power, and intuitively command it to listen to the sound of your deep breathing. Initially it might appear difficult. However, with persistence, it can be done. Try and succeed.

- It helps to chant the Sanskrit word 'Om' while exhaling. This word has a religious meaning as well as a secular significance. Om is the sacred syllable uttered at the beginning and end of a reading of the Vedas, or prior to the commencement of a prayer or sacred work. According to Professor Vaman Shivram Apte, "the word Om first appears in the Upanishads as a mystic monosyllable, and is regarded as the object of the most profound religious meditation. In the *Mandukya Upanishad*, it has been said that this syllable is all that has been, that which is and is to be, and that all is Om, only Om".[2]]
- At this stage of our discourse, we shall limit ourselves to the beauty and significance of the sound of the word 'Om' chanted during

---

2 *The Practical Sanskrit English Dictionary*, 1890, Poona: Motilal Banarsidass, Delhi 2004.

exhalation. You are at liberty to choose any other word that pleases you, but make sure it has the same sonorous effect. While exhaling, chant the word 'Om', stretching the 'o' sound as long as you comfortably can; as 'O o o o o o o o o o o o o o o o o o m', stopping only when your breath runs out. As an alternative, you can chant with a short 'o' sound and elongated 'm' sound: 'Om m m m m m m m m m m m m'. Either way, this chant will help you concentrate on your breath and control the wandering mind.

- Miracle of miracles: with some practice, after some trial and error, the wandering of your mind slows down; nay, it almost totally stops after the first few minutes. This is a state of bliss, *ananda,* a result of meditation. We achieve this by concentrating on our breath and the chant of 'Om'. The chant prolongs the exhalation, and keeps the mind focussed on the breath.
- The meditation technique described above is simple, effective and does not drag religiosity into its application. However, mediation itself is a cause or a principle pursued with zeal or conscientious devotion. It is the greatest source of unadulterated happiness.
- If you have meditated as stated above, you will find your brain lighter, relaxed, and oblivious to your surroundings. Your blood pressure goes

down. Open your eyes slowly in order to get used to your environment. Relax and do not hurry to get up and be busy with your pending assignments. Spend at least ten minutes in this state of calm.

- Try these simple steps and you will find yourself a happy person.

> *Meditation is painful in the beginning but it bestows immortal bliss and supreme joy in the end.*
>
> — Swami Sivananda

8

HAPPINESS FOR THE DEVOUT

> *I believe that the very purpose of our life is to seek happiness. That is clear. Whether one believes in religion or not...*
>
> — Dalai Lama

IN the preceding chapter I wrote of a simple technique of meditation leading to happiness for the non-believers. Almost the same technique is to be followed by the believers with suitable modifications. A good deal is common to the practice in both situations.

For someone who believes in a chosen deity or *ishta devata,* the slight change would be focussing on the deity's image before you begin with the process of meditation. That would have a heightened calming effect on the body because the senses recognise the image of the deity as a source of happiness already.

As you sit in a relaxing pose, focus on your breath, and chant Om as described in greater detail in the preceding chapter, you will feel your body relaxing and calming. At the end of the stipulated half an hour, chanting specific *mantras* would give you an edge over the others.

Chants

- After about thirty minutes, it is time to chant. If you are short of time, shift this segment to the twenty-fifth minute of your meditation schedule.
- You can select your chants. I suggest some which are commonly in use. Repeat each stanza two times in a sing song voice or as suits your temperament.

- ओ३म् भूर्भुवः स्वः
  तत् सवितुर्वरेण्यं भर्गो देवस्य धीमहि।
  धियो यो नः प्रचोदयात्॥
- असतो मा सत् गमय
  तमसो मा ज्योतिर्गमय
  मृत्योर्मा अमृतम् गमय॥
- सर्वे भवन्तु सुखिनः सर्वे सन्तु निरामया;
  सर्वे भद्राणि पश्यन्तु, मा कश्चिद् दुखभाग भवेत्॥
- जीवेम् शरदः शतम्
  पश्येम् शरदः शतम् ।

श्रृणुयाम् शरदः शतम्
प्रबलवाम् शरदः शतम्॥

- बुद्धम् शरणं गच्छामि॥
  धम्मम् शरणं गच्छामि ॥
  संघम् शरणं गच्छामि ।॥

- ओ३म् नमो भगवते वासुदेवाय ॥

- श्रीकृष्ण गोविंद हरे मुरारे
  हे नाथ नारायण वासुदेव॥

- रघुपति राघव राजा राम, पतित पावन सीता राम।
  जय रघुनन्दन जय सिया राम, जानकी वल्लभ जय श्रीराम॥

- हरे कृष्ण हरे कृष्ण कृष्ण कृष्ण हरे हरे।
  हरे राम हरे राम, राम राम हरे हरे॥

शान्ति मन्त्र

- ओ३म् द्यौः शान्तिरन्तरिक्षं

  शान्तिः पृथिवी
  शान्तिरापः

  शान्तिरोषधयः

  शान्तिः वनस्पतयः

  शान्तिर्विश्वेदेवा

  शान्तिर्ब्रह्म

  शान्तिः सर्वं शान्तिः
  शान्तिरेव शान्तिः

  सा मा शान्तिरेधि॥

Followers of other religious faiths and belief systems can replace these with the chants of their choice. It is an established fact that chanting gives you peace of mind or happiness by concentrating your thoughts.

Do not rush up for pending tasks immediately after you open your eyes after meditation and chanting; give your body some time to relax in the prevalent calm atmosphere. You will find your mind and heart at peace and the body relaxed.

> *In meditation the source of strength is one's self. When one prays he goes to a strength greater than his own.*
>
> — Chiang Kai-Shek

9

CONTROL OF MIND THROUGH NON-ATTACHMENT

My mind to me a kingdom is,
Such perfect joy therein I find
As far exceeds all earthly bliss
That god or nature hath assigned.

— Edward Dyer, "My Mind to me a Kingdom is", 1588.

HAPPINESS is ultimately a function of the mind. Writing in *Paradise Lost* (1667), John Milton said that "mind is its own place and in itself can make a heaven of hell and a hell of heaven". Further, "Happiness or misery is in the mind. It is the mind that lives," wrote William Cobbett in *Grammar of the English Language* (1823).

There is no denying the fact that mind is the great lever of all things. All our acts are initiated in the mind. However, the mind can be mischievous, wayward and prankish. Certain misdeeds ordered by the mind bring ruin and unhappiness. Hence, the control and proper application of mind is imperative to lead us in the direction of happiness. This is achieved through developing the attitude of 'non-attachment'.

Indian scriptures and mythological tales have stressed on the fact that the way to ultimate bliss lies through the mind. When one can control the mind, and become non-attached, the pursuit of happiness gets easier. Krishna illustrated this in the following fable taken from the *Shrimadbhagavatam*.

A mendicant's song

Talking to Uddhava, Krishna narrated the following story:

"A Brahmin living in Ujjain had accumulated considerable wealth in trade and farming. However, he was a miser, a lecher and was prone to bouts of anger over minor issues.

"Although a man of means, he never spoke kindly to his kith and kin. He lived an irreligious life, did not utilize his wealth even for his personal comforts. His indifferent attitude made his wife, children, menials and even neighbours unhappy.

None of them wished him well. His indifference was reciprocated with his being totally ignored by everyone.

"Certain adverse circumstances and unexpected turn of events, a few mistakes in trading, some drought that left his fields parched, considerably reduced his wealth. His prosperity vanished and he watched helplessly. The times were bad. A part of his remaining wealth was usurped by relatives; some was stolen by thieves. An accidental fire destroyed his crops and property, and the king's taxes were harsh.

"The Brahmin, thus, found that neither had he enjoyed his prosperity, nor had he accumulated religious *punya*. The closest of his relatives deserted him in this hour of need and penury. He was beset with an avalanche of worries. Loss of wealth made him feel small. He repented over his earlier indifference to the joys of life and his maltreatment of his near and dear ones. When alone, he shed uncontrollable tears. He saw no way out of his mire of sorrow. All the same, he experienced a great degree of detachment."

The repentant man cursed his earlier attitude

"Of what use has been my wealth which I worked so hard to earn?" he argued. "I did not give it away in charity. I did not enjoy my riches. It was plain stupid of me. Perhaps a miser can never be happy.

"That is how life is, probably! Even a tinge of greed mars the purity of a good name and like soot hides the worthy qualities of an accomplished person. He puts in hard work to earn and accumulate wealth, then fears its loss, worries about a theft and suspects everyone else of harbouring evil intentions. Riches split families, take wives away from husbands, make enemies of brothers, and alienate sons and daughters from their parents.

"No wise person gets waylaid by riches. The human body is a means to salvation. I misused it. The result is suffering beyond measure. In my ignorance, I lost years of my life, my wealth and my health. In a one-sided pursuit to amass wealth, I squandered the means with which a discriminating person attains *moksha*. It has been futile.

"I am sure that it is god's grace that today I am a pauper. This abject condition has led me to understand suffering. As a result I have a feeling of immense detachment, of *vairagya*. The latter alone will help me to attain salvation, and cross the ocean of misery that this world is.

"Nothing is lost as yet. Why should I yield to a sense of hopelessness? In my remaining years on this earth, I shall strive for self-realization, be involved in acts of charity, seek spiritual knowledge about Brahman, be truthful, and lead a pious life. I shall devote my time to *tapasya* and live frugally. I am sure God will help me in my determination. He is known to be compassionate."

"Uddhava," observed Krishna, "determined to change and follow the path of truth, the Brahmin from Ujjain destroyed his ego. He unfastened the knot of "I" and "mine", of all the possessiveness that had strangulated his life. He was now at peace with himself. He became a *sanyasi* who vowed not to utter a syllable. He was no longer attached to any place, goods or a person or to any desire for possession and hoarding.

"The Brahmin controlled his mind, senses and his breath. Unhindered by greed and attachment, he wandered all over. He no longer belonged to a place. He lived incognito and managed with whatever food he was offered by *grihasthas* (the householders).

"He had become an *avadhoota*, an ascetic who had renounced all worldly attachments and connections, a naked faqeer who was kicked, rejected and even hurt by all and sundry mean fellows. The passer-by snatched his staff, deprived him of his begging bowl, and even hit him for no reason. They teased him, ignored him and abused him without any knowledge of his past. They provoked him to speak. When he kept quiet, they called him names and called him a fraud.

"They tied him with ropes. If they came to know of his former rich status, they laughed at his misfortune. Sometimes they imprisoned him in a hovel as birds are locked in a cage. He suffered and bore all humiliation without protest.

"Uddhava, the mendicant Brahmin at times had fever and there was none to care for him. However, he had reached such a stage of indifference that the worst of treatment never made him angry. He attributed his suffering to his past deeds and bore it with equanimity. In his mind, at times, he churned over the lessons he had learnt from the various events of his life. Thought he,

"I suffer not because of other human beings, or the gods, this body or my stars. My suffering is not a consequence of my *karma,* or of *kala* (time as a continuing phenomenon). According to the Shrutis and the sages the fault lies with my mind. It is the latter that makes the wheel of joy and sorrow turn on its hub.

"The mind is all powerful. It is the source of the joys of the senses and the tendencies resulting from them. Even the soul becomes ineffective when the mind overtakes our impulses. Rather, to all appearances, it finds expression through the activity of the mind. It is the mind that makes us indulge in wild passion and tie even our soul, which otherwise is unattached.

"The ultimate fruit of doing one's duty, of following the rules as laid down in the scriptures, of the study of the Vedas, of doing good deeds and of living like a celibate, is achieving a peace of mind, a focus in god. The absolute concentration of the mind is *param yoga,* the ultimate objective, the greatest of accomplishments. A mind at peace is the greatest reward of a person's good deeds, even of his generosity. A restless mind, a wandering thought process, a slothful living, show that the individual has not benefited at all from his noble activities.

"It is the mind that controls our senses of pleasure, of experience. The mind is a bully, a frightening giant. It can be our enemy. Its vicious attack cannot be repulsed. It hurts not only the visible body but also the inner self, our emotions. It is a mighty task to overcome its turbulence. Hence this should be the first target for control.

"The unwise do not make this effort. Rather, they give prominence to the body and embark on an ego trip. They differentiate on the basis of visibility and come to grief in the belief that they and the others are different persons. Such persons drown in a pool of absolute ignorance.

"If for the sake of argument we accept that man is himself responsible for his joys and sorrows, then why should the soul be blamed? It is the mortal body that suffers, or enjoys.

"If the *devatas* are responsible for our suffering, why lay the blame at the door of the soul, of our consciousness. The same gods reside in every human being. How then can one look at another angrily?

"If we argue that it is the soul that is the cause for suffering or that partakes of the joys, where does the grievance lie? Well, the soul is ourselves, and not a separate and distinct entity. How can it share the blame and with whom? It is indistinguishable. Any other belief is a mere illusion. This eliminates the possibility of joy or suffering from an outside source. Why be angry and with whom? What is the source of anger?

"If we believe that the source of suffering lies in our stars or in the influence of the planets, how does that affect the soul that is never born, that never dies? Their baleful influence, if any, can only be on the body that is subject to birth and death. Why then get angry with the stars and the planets?

"Further, if the source of our suffering lies in our *karma,* the soul still stays unaffected. A physical body alone can suffer. A substance can be either animate or inanimate. The body in itself is inanimate. The soul that provides consciousness is not subject to variations or adversity. It is only a disinterested witness. It never performs any *karma*. How then can we blame the karma for our suffering and be angry?

"Can *kala* be a source of our suffering or of the joy we experience? How does that affect the soul? *Kala* itself is a variation of the *atma,* the soul. Just as fire cannot burn itself, ice cannot melt ice, *kala* cannot cause pain or suffering to *atma,* it's variant. How then is anger justified against *kala*?

"Our soul is beyond heat or cold, beyond joy or sorrow. It is not affected by different aspects of nature, by *dharma,* actions, by even an infinite substance, relationships or any scents. It is unaffected by duality of any kind. The latter is experienced by the ego which is subject to the illusion of birth and death.

"I shall shed my fear of suffering, of impending calamities and live fearless like the *rishis*. I surrender myself to god and meditate upon Him and obey His guidance."

Continued Shri Krishna,

"Uddhava, once he had lost his riches, the Brahmin of Ujjain no longer suffered. Unattached, he wandered like a *sanyasi*. In spite of being harassed by the passers-by, he stood his ground of noble thought and goodwill towards all. He observed silence and in his heart he sang of me in devotion.

"Uddhava, suffering is an illusion of the mind. This world, the divisions of friends and foes among beings, are a creation of ignorance.

"I ask for surrender of every instinct. I ask for a control of thought. That alone provides peace of mind and stability. This is the essence of all the *yoga*. This *bhikshuka geet,* the song of the mendicant, is the esence of all knowledge, of the knowledge of Brahma."

This is the greatest message for developing an attitude of 'non-attachment'.

> *Our mind is like the mind of a child, dizzy while going round and round playing games. Due to ignorance, our mind, that otherwise is the source of all action and thought, assumes that he is the 'subject', the doer of all deeds. However, that is not so. Krishna alone is mother, father, the soul and the master of all creation. He is the doer. He is the Ultimate Truth.*
>
> — [Extracts from author's *Krishnaleela and Other Tales from Shrimadbhagavatam*]

10

THE UNLIMITED BOUNTY OF NATURE

I love snow, and all the forms
Of the radiant frost;
I love waves, and winds, and storms,
Everything almost
Which is nature's, and may be
Untainted by man's misery.

— P. B. Shelley, *Song,* 1822

Joys of nature

WHY not seek happiness in the unlimited bounty of nature? Nature is everywhere. Its pleasures come free. The rising sun, the full moon in the autumn sky, the rolling waves of the ocean, the fine raindrops, the swaying coconut trees on a beach, a budding lotus in the lotus pond, the red and orange of the gulmohar trees in summer, the yellow bunches on a laburnum tree in May, are all a feast for the eye and an immense source of happiness.

Happiness in smaller doses

While a constant state of bliss is associated with meditation, happiness in smaller doses can be attained in hundreds of other objects in nature. "The investigation of nature," wrote T.H. Huxley (*Administrative Nihilism*, 1871), is an infinite pleasure-ground, where all may graze, and where more they bite, the longer the grass grows, the sweeter is its flavour and the more it nourishes."

Nature satisfies all our senses

"What is this life if full of care,
We have no time to stand and stare?"

I invite you to come out of your home, walk into nature, stand and stare. I promise you an unlimited measure of the cup of happiness.

Nature manifests itself in several ways. I propose to talk to you about those aspects that are familiar to everyone and easily accessible.

MOUNTAINS

The sunrise on the Himalayas

Happiness is a state of mind, no doubt. However, it is an emotion perceived by our senses as well. Sitting in a deck chair with a steaming cup of tea, or wrapped in a cosy blanket at the Kausani Dak Bungalow near Almora in Uttaranchal, I used to sit spell-bound, looking at the sunrays slowly and successively illuminating the Himalayan peaks of Panchachuli, Chaukhamba, Trishul, Nanda Devi, and others, a broad massif of 350 kilometres or more. The permanently snow-bound peaks gradually changed colour from grey to orange to gold and finally to white as the sunrays caressed them. It is a phenomenon repeated every day, barring the raining seasons when the clouds play spoil sport. Such a spectacle that can be seen from hundreds of places wherever there are mountains is an immense source of joy.

In Ranikhet, I used to wander aimlessly on roads and in the valleys surrounded by fragrant pine trees and the tall majestic oaks and deodars. Wild flowers bloomed in every nook and corner. Here, too, the spectacle of sunrise was magnificent and a source of happiness.

Mountain peaks radiating happiness

Mountain peaks are scattered around the world. In order to admire their beauty, you do not have to be a Tenzing Norgay or Edmund Hillary and climb the Mount Everest. For being happy at the sight of a mountain peak jutting into the blue sky, you can look out of an aircraft window flying over the Mount Kilimanjaro or The Matterhorn or from the veranda of a hotel room or roadside in Darjeeling that overlooks Kanchenjunga, world's third highest peak. The architecture of these and other mighty peaks is a work of art. Each such sighting fills you with delight. Going to Srinagar by air, admire the Himalayan peaks on your right. The glorious sight is a perennial source of joy.

FLOWERS

All over the world, several valleys of flowers are scattered between the mountain peaks and are by and large easily accessible. Looked at from the sky, these appear to be colourful designs of a verdant carpet. These natural gardens bloom every season, with big and small colourful flowers, a sight to behold. One feels an upsurge of joy in the body. In the Olympic Mountain of Washington, the visitor can enjoy the sight of asters, lupines and paintbrushes besides several other alpine flowers.

In India, the well-known Valley of Flowers lies in Uttarakhand in the western Himalayas. It covers an area of around eighty-seven square kilometres. Nature's bounty there consists of alpine flowers that bloom from June to October. More than five hundred species of wild flowers grow there. This world heritage site provides happiness to every visitor. The flowers grow in myriad colours; the butterflies going from one flower to another display yet another set of colours and induce joy.

As you trek through the Valley of Flowers, besides the blooms, you can notice waterfalls cascading over rocky boulders, and snow-clad Himalayan peaks. The river Pushpawati divides the valley into two and is in itself a sight to please the senses. Among the flowers you can easily identify lilies, poppy, calendula, daisies, dianthus, geraniums, holly, pansies, zinnia and petunia.

Looking at a little flower growing in your garden or balcony would give you the same sort of delight.

RIVERS

Rivers are a symbol of eternity. On and on they flow, for thousands of kilometres. Some of the happiest moments in my memory are those spent sitting on the banks of the Ganges in Haridwar or at Allahabad.

The Ganga *arti* at Haridwar or at Varanasi attracts flocks of devotees at sunset. It is a heavenly spectacle for the devout and all others. The best hours to sit and relax on the river bank are before sunrise or just around sunset. Close your eyes and listen to the music of the running water, and you will notice your worries flowing away with the water.

John Dyer wrote in *Grongar Hill,* 1726:

"And see the rivers how they run

Through wood and mead, in shade and sun,

Sometimes swift, sometimes slow,

Wave succeeding wave, they go

A various journey to the deep

Like human life to endless sleep."

A river is not just a mass of water flowing to its doomed end in the ocean. All over the world the mighty rivers have provided sustenance to mankind. Cities like Delhi, Varanasi, Kolkata, Paris, London, Moscow and New York are situated on the banks of rivers. River-sidewalk, such as the one on the Seine in Paris, or on the Thames in London, is a source of joy to all those who pass by. The moving sheet of water is a balm to the tired eye. All along the river shores, melodious birds sing 'madrigals'. Along with other spectacles of ships, luxury yachts, fishing canoes on certain river banks, at places one can see the delightful, snow-white egrets wading in the shallows in small groups.

WATERFALLS

Talking of rivers as a source of happiness, one cannot forget the waterfalls, well-known or otherwise, that dot river valleys all over the world. The spectacle of a sheet of water falling hundreds of feet is awe-inspiring. Looking at the broad expanse of the horse-shoe shaped Niagara Falls rolling 176 feet into the gorge, I stood unblinking, spell-bound. The thunderous sound made by the falling water is magnificent. This too is happiness flowing out of intense concentration. In Venezuela, the Angel Falls stumble 3,212 feet down over rocks while Zambia celebrates with the Victoria Falls coming down 355 feet.

THE OCEANS

A sight that overwhelms the senses

Show me a person who is not overwhelmed at the sight of the vast expanse of the sea. I was born far away from any ocean. As I grew up and read about the oceans of the world in my geography lessons, I longed to see one. I was twenty-four when I visited Mumbai for the first time and stood face to face with the Arabian Sea at Marine Drive. A senior colleague-cum-guide told our group who stood watching the August high tides, "This is the ocean. There the waters meet the horizon but that is not the end. There is no wall there. The waters continue and go round the earth touching many countries. The sea, whether in turmoil as at present, or when calm, never fails to delight the heart."

Byron's words describe the happiness that an ocean can bestow:

> "There is a pleasure in the pathless woods,
> There is rapture on the lonely shore;
> There is society, where none intrudes,
> By the deep sea, and music in its roar."
>
> *Childe Harold*, iv, 1818

Colourful skies on the dark blue waters

I have been on many voyages. I have seen massive waves reaching the highest decks of my ship, *Harsha Vardhan* near Madagascar in the Indian Ocean. I have watched with fascination the sunset and sunrise on the ocean waves near the Seychelles Islands. The changing hues of the sky work a spell on the human mind; happiness is born. The effect lasts quite some time. I have taken morning walks on the top deck watching the seas surrounding Singapore, Malaysia, Thailand, Hong Kong and Taiwan in *Super Star Virgo* and other ships. Every moment is full of joy. The cool breeze that blew serenely in my face, the soothing droplets of the ocean water sprinkled on my cheeks and eyes, the sight of charming boats and other magnificent ships, everything added to my stock of happiness.

Herman Melville wrote in *Moby Dick* (1; 1851), "I am in the habit of going to sea whenever I begin to grow hazy about the eyes, and to be over conscious of my lungs." Here the improvement in sight and health is an additional source of happiness.

Just standing and staring on the rising and falling waves inspires in our mind the thoughts of "unpathed waters, undreamed shores" (Shakespeare: *The Winter's Tale,* iv, 1611). Going to sea is like offering a prayer. It brings peace of mind and immeasurable joy. Our imagination can leap as high as possible looking at the snow white foam of the ocean.

Coral and sea shells

Just below the surface or on the shores of an ocean, it is a riot of colours, giving immense happiness to the beholder.

Travelling in motorboats near the Lakshadweep Islands in the Indian Ocean, I have been fascinated by the beds of living colourful coral underneath. Their colours range from red-orange to deep or strong pink or even white. The play of filtering sunbeams makes the coral reefs entrancing to look at.

Worldwide, sea shores are littered with sea shells; collecting them is a simple and rewarding hobby. Shells change their colour according to the climate of the region. Brightly coloured species are produced in warm climates, while shells of subdued colour are produced in cool regions.

Birds on the shores

The sea shores are a favourite with migratory birds and hence a source of delight to the watchers. Twice a year, whole colonies of migrant birds from the tundra and higher lands in the north travel as far as the South America and Africa, to Australia or the Pacific Islands, to hatch and brood a family. If you happen to be in these areas, get a guide to watch the strong gulls and the graceful terns, and look at their wing size, the orange colour of the tern beaks, long and stout legs, and the terns alighting on water to bathe.

> *Impressions on the human mind are like the channel of a stream, deepened by constant flow. The flow, for us, is experience—listening to the wind, feeling the warmth of the sun, watching the play of light on cascading water. All that we have learned makes each new experience richer.*
>
> — "Joy of Nature", The Reader's Digest Association, Inc. 1977

11

THE NIGHT SKY

Twinkle, twinkle, little star!
How I wonder, what you are,
Up above the world so high,
Like a diamond in the sky.

— Ann and Jane Taylor, *Rhymes for the Nursery,* 1806

The starlit canopy of the sky

SITUATED several light years away, all in their different orbits, stars have sparkled and bewitched mankind through ages. Lying on a cot in the dark nights of my home town, more than sixty-five years ago, I used to count the brighter stars in the firmament. However, numbers failed each time the counting started. Whenever a star fell, making an arc over the dome of the sky, there were shouts from all the roofs where others were doing what I was. My fascination with stars grew with age and in 1969, staying at the Eagle Flask guest house at Talegaon near Pune, Mr. Padamsee, the Managing Director of the Company gifted me a tiny booklet on stars.

I spent the next one year lying face up on the roof of my cooperative society building in Mumbai, with my wife Swarn lovingly accompanying me, looking at the constellations and tallying their shapes with the pictures given in the book. Hundreds of hours were, thus, spent in this identification exercise till we could correctly point out the major constellations and their prominent stars. Imagine our happiness!

To admire the glory of the starlit sky, stand in wilderness, away from the city lights and look at the moonless night sky. It is one of the most captivating sights in nature. It is only when you move a little away from a city and steer clear of smoke and pollution that you will be able to see the star-studded spectacle. The human eye cannot comprehend the numbers; but the effort in itself is ecstatic.

However, one can begin in a simple fashion.

Get hold of a book on stars and planets from any bookstore. One such valuable guide is *Stars and*

Planets by Ian Ridpath. Its star charts are provided by the Royal Greenwich Observatory.

You can use a virtual telescope now available on the Internet with most search engines.

Now, where do we begin in this pursuit of happiness in the distant worlds visible to the naked eye as planets and twinkling stars?

I propose to take up a few of the most easily distinguishable constellations and stars visible to the naked eye.

(Each sighting described here, but for the Moon and Venus, relates to 10 p.m. in the northern hemisphere. The constellations and stars continue to be visible for months together till they rise and set in daylight.)

JANUARY 15

Orion

In mid-January, right in the middle of the sky overhead, in the northern hemisphere, appears Orion, the most magnificent of constellations. It is visible from most places on the earth because it is positioned on the celestial equator. It represents a hunter with the right hand raised with a sword or a mace to strike. The body is imagined by two triangles that meet at the waist with three prominent stars making a gem-studded belt. (Mind you, it is all in the imagination of the viewer. However, once you start recognizing Orion, you would always see the hunter in your mind's eye.)

On the hunter's right shoulder, a red supergiant star named Betelgeuse, 430 light years away, shines bright. On his left foot you notice a blue super giant star called Rigel, the brightest star in Orion. Rigel is 770 light years away and is the seventh brightest star in the sky as visible to us.

Pleiades

Mankind has imagined that Orion, the hunter was enamoured of a group of nymphs called the Pleiades, a star cluster in the nearby constellation Taurus. You cannot miss this pretty cluster if you move your eye slightly above and west of the hunter's left shoulder. In the West this cluster is known as the Seven Sisters, daughters of Atlas and Pleione. And as per the Indian mythology, Pleiades is known as Krittikas, who gave birth to Shiva's son Kartikeya.

Sirius

Orion is the beginning of our journey of happiness in the observation of the sky. Looking south, below the right limbs of the hunter, we have Canis Major, a constellation that includes Sirius, the brightest of all the stars. Sirius emits the light of twenty suns with blinding luminosity. It is only 8.6 light years away.

The human eye cannot miss its brilliance. Sirius continues to be prominently visible in February and March as well.

Gemini

Looking north, just near the zenith, slightly to the left above the Orion, you will find Gemini, in the form an inverted U. At the bottom of the 'U', near the zenith, you will find two bright stars, Pollux to the left and Castor to the right. Pollux is one of the twenty brightest stars in the sky, 34 light years away. It is an orange coloured giant. Valmiki in his *Ramayana* has often compared Pollux and Castor (Punarvasu) to Rama and Lakshmana, i.e. inseparable. Gemini is known as Mithuna, meaning a couple or twins in Sanskrit. In the Greek mythology, Gemini represents the twins Pollux and Castor who sailed in search of the Golden Fleece. They were regarded as patron saints of the seafarers.

The easy recognition of this constellation is a source of immense joy. In mid February, Gemini occupies the central space in the area just below the zenith.

Canopus

Looking down south, almost near the horizon, in the January sky, you will notice Canopus, the second brightest star in the sky, a white super giant, 14,000 times more luminous than the sun. It lies 310 light years away and is a part of the constellation Carina. In Indian system, we know this mighty star as Agastya *muni*, named after the sage who played an important role in the *Ramayana* at the time of Rama's decisive battle against Ravana.

Aldebaran

To the west of Orion, slightly above, shines Taurus, the bull at the centre of which lies Aldebaran, a red giant star, easily recognizable to the naked eye. Taurus itself is a magnificent constellation of the zodiac. It is believed that the Greek God Zeus had transformed himself into a bull in order to abduct Princess Europa of Phoenicia. Mission fulfilled, he carried her on his back while swimming to Crete. A fascinating story, is it not? Aldebaran forms the bull's red, bloodshot eye on the right of his forehead.

FEBRUARY 15

Cygnus and Lyra

Near the northern horizon, almost near the centre, one can see the pretty and simple formations of Cygnus and Lyra, both constellations easily identifiable.

Cygnus is a large constellation in the shape of a swan. According to the Greek mythology, Zeus assuming the form of a swan courted the Queen

Leda of Sparta. Their union produced the twins Castor and Pollux as well as Helen of Troy. Cygnus is known as the Northern Cross as well.

Lyra can be recognized by its shape, that of a lyre. The instrument was played by Orpheus, a great musician of the Greek mythology. One cannot miss Vega in Lyra, the fifth brightest star in the sky, with a blue-white hue, and twenty-five light years away.

MARCH 15

Leo and Regulus

Below the zenith, in the centre of the sky, left of Gemini, you can see the well-formed constellation Leo. It is called *Simha* (the lion) in Sanskrit. It has the shape of a lion crouching on its legs, ready to jump. Its most notable star is Regulus, a blue-white star, 77 light years away.

Leo is a large constellation, not easily missed because of its form.

Ursa Major

Look towards the north and just above the zenith you will see Ursa Major, a fascinating spectacle known to every civilization. In Hindu mythology, Ursa Major is known as Saptarishi, the seven great seers of the ancient times, i.e. Marichi, Atri, Angiras, Pulastya, Pulaha, Kratu and Vasishtha.

Ursa Major forms an easily recognizable pattern of a plough and is, therefore, known as 'The Big Dipper' or 'The Plough'. All the seven stars are easily and clearly visible to the naked eye.

Ursa Minor

Just above Ursa Major, in a reverse pattern lies Ursa Minor. Its tail-end star is Polaris, the pole star, the north celestial pole. Polaris is moderately bright and is placed one degree from the North Pole. Since ancient times, sea-farers have found the north direction looking at the Pole Star.

In Hindu mythology, Dhruva, a devotee of Vishnu, was elevated to be the Pole Star, an unchanging position in the heavens.

Both the constellations, Ursa Major and Ursa Minor, like a thing of beauty, are a joy forever to anyone who looks at the northern sky on a moonless night.

APRIL 15

Bootes

Next to the tail of Ursa Major, on the left, spread over the north and the south of the zenith, look for Bootes. It is a well-formed pattern of two triangles joined at their base with their cones pointing away from each other. The lower cone has at its junction Arcturus, the brightest star north of the celestial equator. It is a red giant, and is the fourth brightest star in the sky.

Arcturus is one hundred times more luminous than the sun. In Sanskrit, Arcturus is known as Swati who in Hindu mythology is one of the wives of the Sun god.

Corona Borealis, the Northern Crown

A beautiful semi-circular pattern of seven stars is visible, looking north, left to the upper cone of Bootes. It is said that Corona Borealis represents the crown worn by Princess Ariadne of Crete at the time of her marriage to God Dionysius. The latter threw the crown into the sky where its jewels turned into stars that continue to dazzle.

MAY 15

Spica in Virgo

While you can see Bootes with Arcturus in the middle of the sky, a little down below is the constellation Virgo in which shines Spica, halfway down from the zenith looking south. Virgo is the largest constellation of the zodiac and lies on the celestial Equator next to Leo. Its brightest star, Spica is 260 light years away, and can be easily discerned with the naked eye. It is one of the twenty brightest stars as visible to us.

JUNE 15

Scorpius

None can miss the clear-cut formation of Scorpius with its head and curved tail. The constellation lies south of the zenith and represents the scorpion in Greek mythology that stung Orion to death. In the skies, Scorpius rises as Orion sets. Its brightest star is Antares, easily identified as a jewel in the heart of the scorpion.

Scorpius is a lovely constellation to watch. Its outline is as distinct as that of Orion, Ursa Major or Gemini.

Venus

Often mistaken as a star, Venus is the brightest object in the sky next to the sun and the moon. Venus is a planet of the sun just like the earth. Venus shines bright because of its covering of bright clouds and proximity to earth.

As Venus' orbit lies between the sun and the earth, it is seen either in the morning or the evening sky. It never goes very high in the sky, making it easy to find. Look for the brightest object just after sunset or before sunrise when Venus is positioned to the east or the west of the sun.

In Roman mythology, Venus is the goddess of love and beauty.

Moon

Moon, as we all know, is visible in various shapes and sizes across the month. Whether full or in its phases, it has always been a source of delight to mankind. It is an unearthly thing very close to the earth. While the naked eye can show the smile-like shape or the rounded fullness, a pair of binoculars brings into sharp view its craters, lowlands and uplands. An autumn moon is considered to be the prettiest of sights in the clear sky and is, therefore, an occasion for celebration and feasting. The crescent moon has astonished and delighted mankind since times immemorial. Venus, when visible near the crescent moon, makes a picturesque image – fascinating, riveting and astonishing.

While lovers have delighted in meeting their beloveds under the dark sky studded with the moon, poets also have been taking advantage of the moon and its charm to pour out great verses. John Keats in his *Epistle to my Brother* (1816) says,

> "Or the coy moon, when in the waviness
> Of whitest clouds she does her beauty dress,
> And staidly paces higher up, and higher,
> Like a sweet nun in holiday attire."

And here is Percy Bysshe Shelley's *The Cloud,* listening to the beat of the moon's unseen feet when it dances on the carpet of the clouds:

> "That orbed maiden with white fire laden,
> Whom mortals call the moon,

Glides glimmering over my fleece-like flour
By the midnight breezes strewn;
And wherever the beat of her unseen feet,
Which only the angels hear,
May have broken the woof of my tent's thin roof,
The stars peep behind her and peer."

Sky - A perennial source of happiness

I have given you a slight hint of the delightful heavens visible every night. The return is immediate as well as in perpetuity. Once you get accustomed to looking at the sky and identifying important stars and constellations, your appetite will grow. In looking at and understanding the celestial spectacle of nature, hurry is unwarranted. The panorama does not change every day, although it does alter all the time.

I have highlighted certain stars and constellations according to my deep study, observation and experience of decades. There are many more which are visible to the naked eye. As your appetite grows, you will make your own discoveries and select your own favourites.

My time of choice to look at the sky is very early morning, at least an hour before sunrise. However, the descriptions given above relate to around ten in the evening. Drive away from a city's lights and you will find the spectacle to be overwhelming and astounding.

Visit a planetarium if there is one nearby to partake of the entertaining and educative programmes they hold frequently.

Let not clouds disappoint you, for the stars and planets will continue to glitter.

How beautiful this night! The balmiest sigh
Which vernal zephyrs breathe in evening's ear,
Were discord to the speaking quietude
That wraps this moveless scene.
Heaven's ebony vault,
Studded with stars unutterably bright,
Through which the moon's unclouded grandeur rolls,
Seems like a canopy which love has spread
To curtain her sleeping world.

— Percy Bysshe Shelley, *Queen Mab*, 1813

12

THE JOY OF FLOWERS

To me the meanest flower that blows can give
Thoughts that do often lie too deep for tears.

— William Wordsworth, *Intimations of Immortality*, 1807

Say it with flowers

THE Society of American Florists works with the slogan 'Say it with flowers'. And how true! We send our greetings on birthdays, anniversaries, and weddings by presenting a bouquet of flowers. It is the simplest way of spreading unalloyed happiness. Flowers do not have a voice; and yet, they speak. They speak the language of joy to the onlooker.

Every morning, I spend my walking hour looking at a riot of colours in the blooming garden of The Club. On the backdrop of velvet green leaves, I see bunches of yellow bells; pink, russet and white bougainvillea; white, pink and yellow oleander; the peacock flowers in their pretty orange and yellow shades; crocus lilies; fragrant hibiscus; multi-hued champak blooms in pink, yellow, white and maroon; and the pink lotus opening its folds to greet the morning sun. Watching flowers is as much a source of delight as walking in the fresh air, moving pulleys in the gym or swimming in the turquoise swimming pool with its waves reflecting the sunbeams.

Flowers do not ask for anything in return for their gift of happiness. Theirs' is a totally selfless offering. While the spring sees more blooms than other parts of the year, flowers are present all the year around. That makes them a perennial source of happiness. "Flowers are the sweetest things that God ever made," wrote

H.W. Beecher (*Life thoughts,* 1958). God made them for us, the human beings. He made the flowers bloom so that we could be happy.

I proceed to write about a few flowers where happiness is writ large on their form, on their petals, in their colour, and at times in their fragrance. They bloom all around you. Just get out of your home and stroll in a nearby garden. Happiness flows from these flowers like honey from a honeycomb. Find some time out of your busy schedule to look at these flowers; you will notice the change immediately.

As I elaborate as under, you will realise that these flowers have been enmeshed into our daily lives in various other capacities as well and all major civilisations have understood their importance.

Lotus

Associated with numerous gods such as Vishnu, Brahma and Lakshmi in the Hindu mythology, lotus flowers are seen everywhere, almost fifty species of partially submerged perennials occurring worldwide. The Sanskrit poets compared Krishna's eyes to a budding lotus, calling him Kamala Nayana. We bow at the lotus feet of Hari, His *charana kamala*. From Vishnu's navel sprang the lotus which supported Brahma, the Creator.

The Egyptians grew lotus as long ago as 2000 B.C. The Japanese have long cultivated lotus in water gardens. Mauritius boasts of a lotus pool with huge leaves floating like circular boats.

Called water lilies in the west, the lotus flowers are either day-blooming or night-blooming. The best time to look at the flowers is at sunrise when their charms are on full display. You will be astonished to see various shades to a lotus: pink, purple, and white, among many others. The bed of large bottle green leaves on which they grow is equally delightful to behold.

Lily

Like John Keats' "thing of beauty", a lily flower is "a joy forever". There are more than a hundred varieties of lilies worldwide, with equally attractive names, e.g. Connecticut King, Bright Star, African Queen, Black Beauty, Magic Pink, etc. Their colour, the flowing lines of the petals, the curves of the blooms like those of a curvaceous damsel and eye-catching designs created by the Master Creator arouse in one a pure sense of joy.

Lilies are offered in worship to the Virgin Mary. Wreaths of lilies were laid at the tombs of the Egyptian Pharaohs. Lilies are a heady combination of showy looks and fragrance.

Rose

When one thinks of flowers, rose is inevitably the first name that comes to mind. A garden without rose plants is incomplete, so is human happiness.

In Persia, in the mogul court in India and in the court of English kings, rose was valued for its fragrance, looks and taste.

Roses of various colours are taken as symbols of feeling: red for love, white for peace, yellow for friendship, and so on.

Shakespeare wrote in *The Taming of the Shrew*,

"I'll say she looks as clear
As morning roses newly washed with dew."

The heady fragrance of a rose lifts the mood. Its looks and innate grace of form makes the onlooker happy instantaneously.

Even the names they have been given – e.g. Lovely Lady, Loving Memory, Lavender Jewel, Laughter Lines, Golden Wings, Gentle Touch, Peace, Sweetheart, and Escapade – bring back a horde of happy memories.

Tulip

The tulip fields of Holland, Central Asian countries, in the steppes and the alpine heights, and of Kashmir are a source of delight to the onlooker. Acres and acres of the colourful blooms sway in the breeze. The symmetry of the flowers has to be seen to be believed. Their colour varies from light yellow to blood crimson. The flowers have lovely names, such as Arabian Mystery, African Queen, Angelique, Apricot Beauty, Bird of Paradise and Blue Heron.

Narcissus/ Daffodil

More than a hundred varieties of this flower are grown all over the world. Narcissus flowers have short cup-shaped centres while the daffodils have large trumpet-like centres. Their names are as pretty as the flowers, such as Bridal Crown, Broadway Star, Dover Cliffs, Cool Crystal, Ice Wings, Honey Bird,

Dove Wings, Lemon glow, February Silver, Suzy, Shining Light, Rip van Winkle, Tahiti, Rainbow, Yellow Cheerfulness and Woodland Star.

We rejoice when we look at these flowers. So did William Wordsworth when coming upon "a host of golden daffodils . . . fluttering and dancing in the breeze", he wrote:

"...Continuous as the stars they shine
And twinkle on the Milky Way,
They stretched in never ending line
Along the margins of the Bay:
Ten thousand saw I, at a glance,
Tossing their heads in sprightly dance.

The waves besides them danced; but they
Outdid the sparkling waves in glee;
A poet could not but be gay
In such a jocund company.
I gazed--and gazed--but little thought
What wealth the show to me had brought.

For oft, when on my couch I lie,
In vacant or in pensive mood,
They flash upon that inward eye
Which is the bliss of solitude;
And then my heart with pleasure fills,
And dances with the daffodils."

As the variety of flowers to look at in search of happiness is inexhaustible, so is their fount of delight that never runs dry. Flowers are all around you. Just keep your eyes open. You will be enriched in joy.

Gladiolus

Gladiolus, a species of 180 varieties of perennials, is grown all over the world on rocky slopes, grasslands, and marshy areas, particularly in South and East Africa, the Arabian Peninsula, the Mediterranean, and West Asia. In India, gladioli are planted in every garden that matters. These can also be grown in your home garden. The way the flowers unfurl on showy spikes in myriad colours is as enchanting as are their names: Beauty of Holland, Charmer, Cardinals, Dutch Mountain, Firestorm, Georgette, Happy Time, Queen's Blush, Peace, Sweet Dreams, White Ice and Little Darling. As a lasting cut-flower, these flowers spread a message of joy for days together.

Bougainvillea

Driving from the airport to the City Centre in Nairobi, Kenya, you cannot miss the bougainvillea bushes spread on the road dividers. Their leaves are colourful, ornate and pointed, and their flowers tubular and small, each surrounded by three colourful, petal-like bracts. I have seen, to my delight, the same spectacle in Aligarh or Moradabad in Uttar Pradesh, or in Mumbai where the creeper has been trained to climb on the boundary walls of bungalows. Large bushes grow in each garden and flower many times in a year. Some of its names are Scarlet O'Hara, Miss Manilla, Snow White, Variegata, Tahitian Pink, Texas Dawn, Apple Blossom and Raspberry Ice. More than fourteen species of this evergreen shrub are grown and continue to delight the onlooker.

Jasmine

It is a genus of two hundred or more species grown all over the world in gardens, large or small. The flowers are mostly fragrant and have been used for coiffeur bands by women and wrist bands by the amorous for ages. The lovers spread these flowers on their bed. Some of the most popular varieties in India are *chameli, chandni,* and *motiya*. The snow white flowers, growing on branches full of dark green leaves, shine brilliantly in a moonlit night.

Trees in bloom

For the sheer joy of looking at flowers, I recommend a few trees that grow in many countries and which are rich in bloom, mostly seasonal. The suggestions are inspirational and are not meant to be exhaustive. The reader can make his own choice with ease.

Laburnum/Amaltas

When the sun shines furiously in May and June, the light yellow bunches of the laburnum flowers offer competition to the sunrays. Dr. Subhadra Menon writes in *Trees of India* (Timeless Books, New Delhi), "amaltas appears in a mantle of gold, as though to distract attention from the scorching sun. Its pendant sprays of canary yellow flowers hang down from the tree like chandeliers."

Amaltas is one of the most widespread forest trees of India, Myanmar, Indo-China and the Philippines. Also known as a golden chain, looking at its fragrant flowers hanging in bouquets offers immense delight.

Flame of the Forest/ Palash

Vermilion-red flowers that look like flames of fire are brief in duration. Yet, their glorious sight is unforgettable. In India these flowers are used to make colour for the Holi festival. The palash flowers bloom in clusters at the top of the tree. The velvet buds are deeply bronzed while the petals are orange, the colour of a flame. The tree looks like a forest fire when loaded with flowers.

Jacaranda

I noticed this tree on the roads in Nairobi where its blue-mauve flowers cover entire avenues like a canopy. Its flowers are delicate like a coy damsel and just as lovely. The flowering is from early April to mid-May. In Delhi, the Lodi Garden has quite a few jacaranda trees for the viewer's delight.

Gulmohar

One does not have to travel to the wild to enjoy the celestial beauty of the gulmohar tree. It is everywhere, adorning the avenues and the building compounds. Come summer, its branches are loaded with thousands of orange flowers making the gulmohar probably the most beautiful of the flowering trees. Its flowers are large and showy, with petals done, as if, with a painter's brush. Four of the petals are vivid scarlet and the fifth one is white splashed with scarlet and yellow.

Champa/ Frangipani

It is a tree sacred to Hindus, Muslims and Buddhists. Its flowers are fragrant and of varied colours. Women like to adorn their hair buns with the fragrant champa flowers. The feel of the petals, the subtle colouring of the insides spell magic. The tree itself branches in an artistic fashion; some of the purple flowers feel and look like velvet.

Rusty Shield Bearer

Trees bearing colourful flowers are a rich source of happiness. Look at the Rusty Shield Bearer that blooms every summer. The Mumbai avenues have hundreds of these trees lined up for your delight.

Kachnar

Kachnar or Bauhinia grows all over India. It blooms in December when its large, sweet-scented flowers, present a spectacle of hundreds of butterflies. Its blossoms are like those of an orchid in purple-blue, white, lavender, or magenta colours.

Cassias

In the spring look for Cassias or pink shower for numberless tiny flowers making a crown. The flowers look like rubies set against a green background. The flowers can be white, yellow or pink.

Hibiscus

Hibiscus, known as the queen of shrubs, grows all over the world. In India, hibiscus flowers are offered in worship. Some of the varieties are fragrant but most of them are not. The flowers open in the morning and are dead by evening, having scattered their splendour for our delight. The flowers bloom in blood red, pink, yellow and white shades.

The list of flowers that can make one happy is endless. Our pursuit of happiness becomes easy because nature gave us the wealth of trees and flowers. The spectacle of the flowering trees come without a cost. All the year round, some tree or the other is blooming and spreading its canopy of happiness. Go, snatch a handful of joy!

> *Under the greenwood tree*
> *Who loves to lie with me,*
> *And tune his merry note*
> *Unto the sweet bird's throat?*
>
> — William Shakespeare,
> *As You Like It*, 1600

13

BIRD WATCHING

Behold the merry minstrels of the morn,
The swarming songsters of the careless grove,
Ten thousand throats that, from the flowering thorn,
Hymn their good God and carol sweet of love.
— James Thomson, The Castle of Indolence, 1748

Birds have always been with us

OUR familiarity with birds, the colours of their feathers and their vibrant sounds starts at a very young age. There must have been numerous times when you have woken up to the chirruping of birds.

To give you an instance of the familiarity of humans with birds and how it begins, let me share a personal experience. When our first child arrived, we lived in a first floor house in Meerut near Delhi. A wizened old maid looked after the baby. She sat with the infant in her lap and called the house sparrows saying, "*Bittu ki chirayia, aa, aa, aa*" It can roughly be translated as "come, come, Bittu's sparrow".

Arvind, our infant, nicknamed 'Bittu', used to shriek with delight looking at the tiny birds coming to pick the grain offered by the maid.

Happiness in the music of the birds

There have been many who believed that the music from humans began in our effort to mimic the birds' songs. In the recorded history of music, ancient as well as modern, hundreds of sounds have been produced in voice or through musical instruments to copy or improve upon the notes produced by different birds at dawn or otherwise, to attract a mate or to keep a predator away or to raise an alarm.

A bird's whistle may be much louder and more like a shriek when it has to frighten an enemy. During courtship, the song differs from moment to moment, from urgent calls to intimate cooing. We, in our music, have followed the same pattern.

The morning hours

Bird watching is a source of happiness at all times. However, it is the morning time when the birds really come alive.

It is remarkable how each bird sings his own tune. Not all their calls are delightful. However, those which are melodious have become a part of human poetry and literature.

Asian Koel

Every morning, as I start my walk in The Club garden just around dawn, the bird orchestra starts its merry tune. Each one tries to outdo the others. I can hear the Asian *koel,* the Drongo cuckoo, *papeeha* (the brain-fevered bird), the sparrows and, of course, the crows. The sound that gives the greatest joy is that of the *koel,* although after making its presence known through its loud and melodious song for about four months beginning with the onset of spring, the bird stays silent for the remaining months of the year.

The koel's call begins with a low *kuoo, kuooo*; rises in scale with each successive note; reaches fever pitch at the seventh or eighth, and breaks off suddenly. In a moment it starts again and, thus, goes on. The sound is melodious to the ears and has been celebrated in words, music and dance. It is associated with the joy and arrival of the spring.

Papeeha/ Pied Cuckoo

The *papeeha* has been celebrated by the Hindi poets in thousands of lyrics. The sound *'pee'* which the *papeeha* repeats, literally, means a lover or a husband. This pretty bird screams *piu, piu, piu* as if in delirium almost throughout the day. Once you have identified this sound, you cannot miss it.

The bird song will be different with different birds and most birds are confined to certain regions. Please seek assistance from a knowledgeable person in your locality or a guide book on local birds. However, even if you do not recognise the birds, you cannot miss the simultaneous cooing and chirping of these birds every morning. This medley of music has to be heard to be appreciated.

Skylark

When Percy Bysshe Shelley wrote 'To the Skylark', he tried to find the secret of the bird's melodious voice. The joy of listening to the bird's music is brought out in the first stanza itself:

> "Hail to thee blithe spirit!
> Bird thou never wert,
> That from heaven, or near it,
> Pourest thy full heart
> In profuse strains of unpremeditated art..."

Shelley calls the bird "an embedded joy, shrilling delightfully". He further writes:

"...From rainbow clouds there flow not
Drops so bright to see,
As from thy presence showers a rain of melody..."

According to Salim Ali, the song, delivered on the wing, is the skylark's chief claim to distinction. "From the ground the bird springs almost vertically upwards on fluttering wings: rising higher and higher till it becomes a speck in the sky. It pours forth a deluge of spirited, melodious warbling, often for ten minutes at a stretch." (*The Book of Indian Birds*, 2002.)

Peacock: a symbol of extravagant beauty

A peacock feather is a masterpiece of design. Notice the dancing peacocks wooing their mates in Vrajabhoomi near Mathura or in Jaipur City Palace or almost anywhere you can. The iridescence in the feathers is a result of pigments overlaid with diffractive coatings that add luminosity. Notice the bird's glistening blue neck and breast, its sharp triangular crest and the enormous spread of its tail. The number of feathers in a peacock's fan can be anywhere around two hundred. It is the constellation of eyes in the fan that makes it stand out and attract the female; the larger the number of eyes, the greater is its attraction for the hen.

Krishna, the beloved blue god of many a people, loved to dress a peacock feather in his headband. For his devotees across the world, the peacock feather is a sign of his presence and, therefore, a reason for rejoicing. A dancing peacock reminds them of their dancing god.

Wood Duck

The colour palette used by nature for this duck has produced enchanting results. The head has the shape of a green Napoleon hat white stripes. The top coat is dark green and the breast is mottled maroon. All this is highlighted by a light yellow belly.

Flamingo

The flamingo has looks and features that are a balm to the eyes. Look at them assembled in marshes at Sewri in Mumbai or at Lake Naivasha in Kenya. Admire their rose-white plumage, black and scarlet wings, large, downward-curved pink beak and long legs. In India, they are commonly known as Rajhans, the royal bird. When a flamingo takes off, one can look at its long outstretched legs, neck, and the black-bordered brilliant scarlet wings. Looking at the birds amassed in thousands at Sewri, Lake Naivasha is an exhilarating experience.

Parrots

This is one bird you just cannot miss for the beauty of its feathers and for its friendly temperament. Parrots, along with ravens and magpies are among the most intelligent of birds, and the ability of some species to imitate human voice has made them extremely popular with us all.

By and large, parrots are green with highlights of blue, red and yellow. Parrots are social birds and often move in pairs. The birds are highly vocal, chattering endlessly.

Swans, Geese and Ducks

This is another group of birds that is highly visible. They have been hunted, chased for sport and domesticated. In Sanskrit literature, a lovely maiden's slow and meandering gait is often compared to that of a tip-toeing swan. Their charming form and their cluck-clucking noise has influenced art, music, dance and song.

Bar-headed goose is another lovely species made immortal in Sanskrit literature as *chakravaka* or *rajhans*. Grey, brownish and white in colour, there are two distinctive broad, black bars across their nape. The beauty of its feathers is manifested when the bird flies up to join a migrating flock.

Pigeons

There is no place on earth except Antarctica which has been not inhabited by pigeons. Their colour, form, feather design are splendid. In India it has been a hobby of the rich as well as the poor to keep, breed and fly pigeons for seriously competitive fights. Some of the most beautiful pigeons are the African Green Pigeon, the Victoria crowned pigeon, the Magnificent fruit dove, the common Rock dove seen almost everywhere, and the European turtle dove. The Victoria crowned pigeon is the cutest of all and is probably the largest of the species. It has a magnificent crest which it uses to great effect during courtship.

Most of the birds sit and live on tree tops. The tree branches and their leaves make visibility difficult. However, if you persist, you can catch glimpses of them with ease. I have had the privilege of watching the courtship between a pair of koels sitting on nearby branches, just a foot apart. I stood still listening to an exchange of loving messages in short and sweet notes. They did not fly away. I stood transfixed and felt happy and lucky.

The colours and plumes

Our pursuit of happiness in the world of birds leads us to look at their form which includes exotic colour combinations and shapes of feathers. Look at them. Listen to their music. You will always return richer and happier.

Birds have inspired a lot of art. Their mysteries and physical beauty have nagged painters and poets. But the art to which birds have contributed the greatest inspiration is music.

— Bruce Brooks, *On the Wing,* 1989

14

LAUGHTER, THE RECIPE FOR INSTANTANEOUS HAPPINESS

In laughter there is always a kind of joyousness that is incompatible with contempt or indignation.

— Voltaire, *L'enfant prodigue,* 1736

ABOUT fifteen years ago, during our morning walk, my friend and companion Dr. Madan Kataria casually suggested that we stand in a corner and laugh. Laughter for its own sake, without provocation or without any reason. It was an enchanting suggestion. We collected three more friends, stood under a banyan tree and started laughing loudly. The passers-by in the garden stopped, looked at us, smiled or made faces. Barring a few, they shrugged and continued with their stroll. We continued assembling every day, made delightful and pure laughing noises. With each passing day, more and more members joined the nascent Laughing Club. Today it is a worldwide movement led by Madan, the Messiah of laughter and happiness. Each morning, the garden below my house where we had started the movement, resounds with peals of laughter at 7 a.m. Our tiny Laughter Club has become a worldwide movement for multiplying happiness under Dr. Kataria's stewardship.

He who laughs, lasts

Laughter is an eternally fresh source of happiness. Writing in *The Spectator*, Joseph Addison wrote on 24 April 1711, that "man is distinguished from all other creatures by the faculty of laughter". Nicolas Chamfort went a step further and opined that "the day most wholly lost is the one on which one does not laugh" (*Maximes et Pensées*. c. 1785).

Why is there so much stress on laughter being a distinguishing quality of human beings? It is because pure laughter, not the sneering and contemptuous variety, indicates the emotion of joy in its recognizable and popular form. It was the function of the court jester to raise a laugh for the king. Men like Birbal, one of the gems of Akbar's court, made the king laugh at the most solemn occasions with wit, pun or mimicry. Peals of laughter arose on their comments, resulting in a feeling of happiness all around. Hamlet called a jester "a fellow of infinite jest, of most excellent fancy."

The magic of nothingness

When we laugh for laughter's sake, we enlarge our vision, our consciousness to partake of the magic of nothingness. A human being indulging in innocent laughter forgets himself and goes into a sort of trance. That is a facet of meditation. Once he forgets worry, misery, enmity, anger, sickness, and jealousy, he commands a fountain of pure joy and unadulterated happiness.

As Dr. Kataria puts it, "When you are happy, you make yourself laugh. Conversely, when you laugh, you are making yourself happy". In my view, forgetfulness is the key to this state of happiness.

The technique

Laughter for its own sake costs nothing. Stand anywhere, preferably in the open or in your home facing a window. Relax and start laughing, "Ha ha ha ha —".

Inhale deeply; exhale fully. Be in control of your breath. Soon you will feel light, the burden of existence lightened, and spiritually uplifted; therefore, happy. Catherine Fenwick puts it meaningfully: "Your body cannot heal without play. Your mind cannot heal without laughter. Your soul cannot heal without joy." The exercise of innocent laughter lights the Sun of happiness. Laugh, laugh and laugh. Laugh out loud, forgetting all worries, without a single upsetting thought to bar you. "Ha ha ha ha –"

In high volume, in soft tones, loudly or in whispers; but laugh you must. Therein lies happiness.

When you laugh, you get a glimpse of God – Merrily Belgum

Gautama Buddha understood the importance and value of laughter as a source of happiness. He wrote, "When you realize how perfect everything is, you will tilt your head back and laugh at the sky."

Laughter has simultaneously a physical manifestation and a spiritual connect. Rabbi Sydney Mintz has put it in a scientific context: "when you laugh, aside from the endorphin rush, there is also a spiritual opening. You are not so tight yourself. That opening I have found to be a real gift, in people being able to absorb spirituality."

Banish the fear of transitoriness

"Life is short and time is fleeting", wrote Longfellow. Add to this realization, Will Roger's advice: "We are all here for a spell. Get all the good laughs you can." Therefore, in order to get over the fear of transitoriness, laugh today, laugh tomorrow and day after. Says that great master of laughter, Charlie Chaplin, "To truly laugh, you must be able to take your pain and play with it."

Happiness, which we all want to achieve is after all, the reverse of pain. Overcome pain through laughter/ medicine/ or meditation. A moment of happiness is born.

I have had several discussions with Dr. Kataria about his experiences with developing laughter as a therapy for good health and all round well-being resulting in happiness. He counts the benefits of unprovoked laughter on his fingertips. I recount his words in my language.

It has been observed in several medical studies that watching comedies, animal and cartoon movies, listening to jokes, etc., help in the recovery of sick persons. Do not treat laughter as an external and boisterous display of emotion. Laughter is happiness personified. It activates positive chemistry within the body. It brings about hormonal changes for the better.

Dr. Kataria adds that several bursts of laughter gradually lower blood pressure. He has devised varieties of laughter in the form of exercises which involve mouth, lungs and stomach, and back. He says that laughter burns as many calories as cycling. Researchers motivated by the philosophy of the Laughter Club have found that laughter releases endorphins that relieve pain in a natural way. Dr. Kataria stresses that uninhibited laughter relieves stress, dissolves pent-up emotions and adds to brain power.

I offer to the reader some delightful quotes in praise of laughter. The underlying message is the same everywhere: laughter induces happiness.

- "A good laugh is sunshine in the house." – William M. Thackeray.
- "A smile starts on the lips; a grin spreads to the eye; a chuckle comes from the belly. However, a good laugh bursts forth from the soul, overflows and bubbles all around." – Carolyn Birmingham.
- "Always laugh when you can. It is cheap medicine." – Lord Byron.
- "Keep a sense of humour. It doesn't mean you have to tell jokes. If you can't think of anything else, when you're my age, take off your clothes and walk in front of a mirror. I guarantee you'll get a laugh." – Art Linkletter.
- "As soap is to the body, so laughter is to the soul." – A Jewish proverb.
- "Earth laughs in flowers." – Ralph Waldo Emerson.

- "He deserves Paradise who makes his companions laugh." – *Koran*.
- "I was irrevocably betrothed to laughter, the sound of which has always seemed to me to be the most civilized music in the world." – Peter Ustinov.
- "If you become silent after your laughter, one day you will hear God also laughing, you will hear the whole existence laughing, trees and stones and stars with you. – Osho.
- "Laughter is a form of internal jogging. It moves your internal organs around. It enhances respiration. It ignites great expectations." – Norman Cousins.
- "Laughter is the sun that drives winter from the human face." – Victor Hugo
- "Laughter serves as a blocking agent. Like a bullet-proof vest, it may help protect you against the ravages of negative emotions that can assault you in disease." – Norman Cousins.
- "No matter what your headache may be, laughing helps you forget it for a few seconds." – Red Skeleton.
- "Prepare for mirth, for mirth becomes a feast." – William Shakespeare.
- "Remember this: very little is needed to make a happy life." – Marcus Auralius.

- "The best way to cheer you is to try to cheer someone else." – Mark Twain.
- "Think of all the beauty still left around you and be happy." – Anne Frank
- "True humour springs more from the heart than from the head; it is not contempt, its essence is love." – Thomas Carlyle.
- "I have not seen anyone dying of laughter, but I know millions who are dying because they are not laughing." – Dr. Madan Kataria.
- If you are happy and people around you are not happy, they will not allow you to stay happy. Therefore, much of our happiness depends upon our ability to spread happiness around us. – Dr. Madan Kataria

15

CHARITY, A FOUNTAIN OF JOY

> *Spending money on others might represent a more effective route to happiness than spending money on oneself.*
>
> — Professor Elizabeth Dunn, University of Columbia

Charity is twice blessed

Charity, like the quality of mercy, in Shakespeare's words, is twice blessed: "It blesseth him that gives and him that takes". The blessing in the case is the augmentation of the sum total of happiness in the heart of the giver and the joy of possessing what he needed in the mind of the recipient. In my scheme of things, charity makes others happy in so many ways as illustrated in succeeding paragraphs. However, the donor gets much more. The *Qur'an* recognized this fact in the following words:

> "The likeness of those who spend their wealth in the way of Allah, is as the likeness of a grain [of corn]: it grows seven ears, and each ear has a hundred grains. Allah gives manifold to whom He wills."

India has had a tradition of spreading happiness through charity through the ancient, medieval and the modern times.

The Birla family has been an ace performer in spreading happiness via charity. They have set up dozens of *dharmashalas* where free lodging and meals are available to anyone. As a student in Delhi, I have enjoyed these facilities in the lodgings attached to the Lakshmi Narayana temple. My friend and former colleague, Ram Niwas Lakhotia, invested a large part of his life's savings in establishing a *dharmashala* at Ajmer in his father's memory. Till recently, more than a hundred thousand travellers had availed of its free facilities.

I know of a family living at Juhu, Mumbai, whose charitable activities have spread happiness all around without discrimination. The patriarch, Mahavirprasad Saraf has established a foundation that has installed 16,355 concrete, three-seater benches on the footpaths on the public roads, gardens, the railway platforms, in hospitals, old age homes, orphanages, in universities, schools and colleges, in cremation grounds and even railway stations for public use. He gets nothing out of it except happiness while the users, the tired and lonely, quite often hungry passers-by sit on these benches to rest, relax, break a journey or just take a meal. In a city like Mumbai, thousands come from the hinterland daily in the pursuit of their dreams. Quite a few film stars of today spent their initial days on the foot paths. Such concrete benches are a gift for the lonely and the homeless.

Writes Mahavirprasad in a souvenir: "I feel happy and satisfied when I see people sitting on the benches donated by me. It is heartening to see students studying on our benches, old people finding comfort in each others' company, the tired layman relaxing. The commuters get relief and the love birds use them as a meeting point."

Needless to say, these concrete benches generate more happiness in a large, amorphous mass of human beings than can be measured.

Mahavirprasad has been innovative in his charity projects. Safe drinking water fountains have been installed at railway stations, in orphanages, Court compounds, and in schools and colleges. For senior citizens, he has built homes for free stay. He has constructed reading rooms for them, too. His trusts have constructed public toilets throughout Mumbai. They have also established colleges to promote women's education. For the handicapped persons, Saraf's trusts have set up public call booths, given them wheel chairs, digital hearing aids, and walking sticks; sewing machines have been given to needy women.

Another charity-minded businessman donated a few acres of land in another Mumbai Suburb to set up a school for girls. Today, the organization he set up runs fourteen colleges where more than ten thousand students get quality education. One can assess the happiness generated by the initial effort in the students who study in these well-funded and well-furnished schools and colleges with playgrounds, laboratories and hostels. It all started as charity.

Charity makes you feel better

According to BBC News (20 March 2008), Canadian research suggested that "it is not having lots of money that makes us happy – it is spending it on others." The research was conducted by a team from the University of British Columbia. They found that staff that got bonuses and spent some of the extra money on others were happier than those who spent their bonuses on themselves.

Professor Elizabeth Dunn, who led the research, said: "We wanted to test our theory that how people spend their money is at least as important as how much money they earn." She added: "Regardless of how much income each person made, those who spent on others reported greater happiness, while those who spent more on themselves did not."

Each one of us has felt joy in giving in some way or the other. The ancients knew of this truth. It is written in *Deuteronomy* XXIV, 19, c. 650 B.C.:

"When thou cuttest down thy harvest in thy field, and hast forgot a sheaf in the field, thou shalt not go again to fetch it. It shall be left for the stranger, for the fatherless, and for the widow; that the lady of thy God may bless thee in all the work of thine hands."

Charity connects you to God and makes you blissful

Happiness is godliness and the divine manifests as joy in our hearts. God is not just *ananda* but *param ananda,* not just bliss but absolute bliss. Thomas Gray wrote of the poor priest in the "Elegy Written in a Country Churchyard", 1750,

"Large was his bounty, and his soul sincere,
Heaven did recompense as largely send;
He gave to misery [all he had] a tear,
He gain'd from Heaven ['twas all he wish'd]
A friend."

The Indian tradition

India has had a long tradition of being charitable without boasting of one's deeds. Writing of King Dileep in the *Raghuvamsham*, Kalidasa says,

> "Dileep was learned, yet he never boasted about it.
>
> He was mighty, yet he forgave his enemies.
>
> He was charitable.
>
> However, he never looked forward
>
> To being acknowledged as such." [1.22]

This self effacement is the source of immense happiness.

Of what use is wealth, if not given away?

More than two thousand years ago, Bhartrihari wrote in the *Nitishatakam*:

Wealth moves in three ways:

1. Charity
2. Enjoyment
3. Wasteful spending, emptying the coffers

Those who are neither charitable nor spend on their happiness, certainly indulge in wasteful spending and lose everything [43].

In the 71st verse, Bhartrihari wrote:

1. Those who benefit others are naturally humble.
2. They are like a tree that bends low when it is heavy with fruit.
3. They are like the new water-laden cloud that comes down to shower rain on the earth below.

The charitable and merciful do not need ornaments to adorn them with, wrote the king. Their hands do not need golden bangles. It is charity that lends them lustre (*Nitishatakam*, 72).

The good and saintly are ever ready to benefit others. They do not wait for entreaties.

1. They are like the sun which makes lotuses bloom.
2. They are like the moon that shines so that water lilies spread their petals.
3. They are like the cloud that showers rain upon the earth without a prayer (*Nitishatakam*, 74).

> *The one who serves others is the richest. When all the powers that are within are used for the benefit of the self and others, they tend to multiply. So the one who continues to serve others continues to become rich.*
>
> — *Anonymous*